Putting the Pieces Together

Putting the Pieces Together

A Systems Approach to School Leadership

Lee A. Westberry

ROWMAN & LITTLEFIELD
Lanham • Boulder • New York • London

Published by Rowman & Littlefield
An imprint of The Rowman & Littlefield Publishing Group, Inc.
4501 Forbes Boulevard, Suite 200, Lanham, Maryland 20706
www.rowman.com

6 Tinworth Street, London SE11 5AL, United Kingdom

British Library Cataloguing in Publication Information Available

Library of Congress Cataloging-in-Publication Data

Names: Westberry, Lee A., 1969- author.
Title: Putting the pieces together : a systems approach to school leadership / Lee A. Westberry.
Description: Lanham, Maryland : Rowman & Littlefield, 2020. | Includes bibliographical references. | Summary: "This book will describe two of the four major systems needed to effectively lead a school and move the needle on student achievement"—Provided by publisher.
Identifiers: LCCN 2020007479 (print) | LCCN 2020007480 (ebook) | ISBN 9781475854015 (cloth) | ISBN 9781475854022 (paperback) | ISBN 9781475854039 (epub)
Subjects: LCSH: Educational leadership—United States. | School management and organization—United States. | Academic achievement—United States.
Classification: LCC LB2805 .W464 2020 (print) | LCC LB2805 (ebook) | DDC 371.2—dc23
LC record available at https://lccn.loc.gov/2020007479
LC ebook record available at https://lccn.loc.gov/2020007480

This book is dedicated to my husband Danny and my children Warner and Sophie who demonstrated immense patience with me while I spent innumerable weekends writing. I love you all and pray you will continue to show the same patience as I continue my writing endeavors.

Contents

Contents

Ian

Keilya

Jennifer S

Sheldon B

Ashland

Acknowledgments

I would like to acknowledge my youngest daughter, Sophie Westberry, who created the cover art. Such a talented thirteen-year-old!

I would also like to acknowledge my colleagues Dr. Kent Murray and Dr. Mina Schnitta who provided valuable feedback on such a tight schedule.

Introduction

We hear all of the time how the education system and the demands of the system on teachers, administrators, and students have changed so much over the last twenty years. In fact, education seems to remain in a state of change continually. Although these changes make it difficult for parents to know how to help their children, the changes make it as difficult, if not more so, on teachers in the classroom.

Moreover, how does a building-level principal manage all of the daily demands of schools as well as the local, state, and national changes while remaining the leader of the school? Yes, principals must be the instructional leaders of their schools, stay ahead of the changes to come, all the while managing the changes as they come. Sounds like a tongue twister, right? Imagine trying to accomplish all of this without a plan.

The answer lies in the systems that a principal has in place. Systemic approaches are a principal's best friend. Without these systems, principals find themselves barely keeping their heads above water and continually putting out fires. In the latter scenarios, principals can't lead. There are many systems needed to make a school truly successful. *Putting the Pieces Together: A Systems Approach to School Leadership* will outline two of the four large systems that must operate simultaneously in order to successfully lead a school in the constant state of flux: the instructional system and the student support system. *The Final Pieces: A Systems Approach to School leadership* will address the teacher support system and the school culture system. Although there are many more that must exist, like building maintenance, cafeteria needs, and so on, the aforementioned four systems help principals truly lead versus manage and survive.

Chapter 1

Laying the Foundation

A Systems Approach

Recognizing the need is the primary condition for design.

—Charles Eames

One must begin examining school leadership with a systems approach. Systems provide a strong foundation and structure for all school operations. Without a system, principals are often left to continually put out fires and solve problems, never really undertaking the true task of instructional leadership. Let's be honest. When do they have time? That is the number one reason given for not leading instructional initiatives—time. District initiatives and state and federal directives are very time consuming and are constantly evolving. Each year more is added to the plates of principals. Because of this, the principalship has changed drastically in the last ten to fifteen years. Principals have been forced to become jugglers with far too many balls in the air, and true instructional leadership and some of the other important systems are often balls that are dropped.

Principals don't intentionally drop these balls, but the time it takes is often seen as a luxury rather than a necessity. The increasing demands placed on principals contribute to the principal turnover rates the nation is experiencing (Fuller, 2012; Tyre, 2015). The cost of principal turnover is higher than the monetary cost. Teachers, students, and communities are impacted from inconsistency in leadership. Teacher turnover is higher, and student achievement drops as a result of principal turnover (Bartanen, Grissom & Rogers, 2019).

A recent estimate is that it takes $75,000 to recruit and train a new principal, and nearly 50 percent of principals in some areas leave after their first three years (Granata, 2019).

Additionally, some principals look to central services to provide instructional leadership, not understanding that allowing central service to direct instruction in school buildings serves to undermine the principal's leadership.

While principals try to navigate the sea of change and ever-increasing demands, many deterrents exist to developing a systems approach. These so-called deterrents exist naturally and consume so much time that principals often cannot see that a systems approach would help to manage and lead more effectively.

DETERRENTS TO SYSTEMS APPROACHES

Personnel Changes

Each year, educators are faced with change. In fact, the only thing constant in education is change. Our students' and families' needs change with the world economy and family structure degeneration. Changes come from federal and state legislation each year with new administrations. At the district level, changes trickle down from the state as well as with new district leadership. Superintendents come and go, and with them comes change.

According to Riddell (2018), the average tenure of a superintendent is six years; however, women superintendents' tenures are approximately fifteen months shorter, and tenures are three and a half years shorter in districts with high poverty. Imagine new initiatives with new priorities every few years. Don't forget the district restructuring and new personnel that come with every change in district leadership as well.

School board members can be elected or appointed, based on the district. Traditionally, school board members serve four-year terms which are staggered; so, there are openings every two years (SCBSA, 2017). Again, new board members have new ideas of governance and the roles of members. More change can be introduced, as board members set policies for districts. For example, a South Carolina (SC) district just set a policy for random drug testing of personnel as well as new staff leave policies. These policies can impact the morale and personnel management systems in a school.

A Texas study (Fuller, 2012) showed that principals, like superintendents, do not stay put either. Principal turnover creates teacher turnover as well. The twenty-one-year study showed that only half of middle school principals remained in the same school for three years, and the average tenure of a high school principal was just three years. Most Texas high school principals never saw a class graduate from beginning to end. Think about the change for teachers and students. Think about the impact on the community and school culture.

State and Federal Mandates

Once you consider personnel changes, you have to also consider state and federal changes. Every year, legislatures are inundated with lobbyists who are advocating for some change. Each new U.S. president has an agenda, and education has become a hot topic in the past few administrations.

All of these external pressures create change in our school systems, and principals have to figure out how to make the changes work within their buildings with the least amount of disruption and to the benefit of the staff and students.

This is not to say that the mandates are not good ideas on merit; however, schools have become responsible for teaching so much more than the subjects taught in school. Schools are now responsible for teaching character education, which has taken on a new life with anti-bullying laws across many states; internet safety, with the advent of more technology in education; soft skills training, with pressures from employers to have a ready workforce, and so on.

The list goes on and on, but none of these areas are in the state standards that are required to be taught and tested. See figure 1.1 for just a few examples of new mandates in SC schools.

Year	Law	Initiative	Impact
2016	SC Code of Laws 59-32-5 Comprehensive Health Act	CPR/AED Training	All high school students must receive instruction in cardiopulmonary resuscitation and awareness of the use of automated external defibrillators at least once during four years in school
2015	SC Code of Laws 59-155-10 SC Read To Succeed Act 284	Literacy Instruction and Intervention	All SC teachers and administrators must take a series of educator in-service courses. Instructional time is outlined as well as interventions to include: required screeners multiple times per year, summer reading camps, 3rd grade retentions, state reading plans, etc.
2015	SC Code of Laws 59-29-240 James B. Edwards Civic Education Initiative	Civics Exam	All SC high school students must take a civics exam when enrolled in the required course American Government.
2012	SC Code of Laws 59-26-110 Jason Flatt Act	Youth Suicide Prevention	All SC teachers must undergo 2 hours of youth suicide prevention training and it must be renewed every 3 years.

Figure 1.1   **State Mandates in SC Schools.** *Source:* www.scstatehouse.gov

Think about figure 1.1 and the vast number of implications. Now, think about the time it takes to effectively and efficiently plan for and execute each of these mandates. The following is one example:

For the portion of the Comprehensive Health Education Act that addresses CPR/ AED training, principals have to set up schedules to accommodate CPR/AED training for all high school children at least once. Depending on the size of the school, this could be a monumental task. Think about the questions that need to be answered in order to accommodate this mandate:

1. What is the curriculum to be used?
2. Who is going to teach the curriculum?
3. What training do teachers need?
4. Who will provide the training for teachers?
5. What is the schedule of this training?
6. When will the curriculum be taught?
7. What grade level will receive the instruction?
8. Who will provide the equipment needed?
9. Who will fund the equipment needs?
10. How does a school track the completion of this student-training?
11. How does a school manage students who transfer into the school?
12. Who reports this information?
13. How is the information to be used?
14. How is the public informed about the new program and the need for it?
15. How are students with special needs managed in this program?

These are just a few of the questions that need to be answered fully before implementing this mandate. Not to mention, teachers get very upset when they lose instructional time from their already tight schedules. You would think that the simple solution to aforementioned question two would be physical education (PE) teachers, right?

In SC, all high school students are required to take one PE class in order to graduate. Physical education teachers are charged with teaching PE and health. Seems logical. However, many students take JROTC or Marching Band in lieu of a PE class, and this is allowed by the state.

Also, many students fulfill the state PE and health graduation requirement through virtual school. This may sound odd. How does a student take PE virtually? Well, it happens frequently when students cannot fit all of the courses needed in their schedules. So, this one situation muddies the waters a bit from the logical solution.

Again, a lot of planning has to occur and many problems solved in order to fulfill a mandate that does not affect student achievement results one bit. So, how does a principal manage the barrage of change and remain a leader. Yes, a leader must manage and lead. We have many principals who are great managers but not leaders. An instructional leader who cannot manage operations of a school will also struggle to be effective.

A true educational leader must be able to do both: manage the day-to-day functions of a school and serve as the instructional leader. That is not to say that these same principals who become managers are not, in fact, capable of leading.

The truth is, once a principal is hired, that principal often times starts the great adventure in survival mode. Too often, when principals are asked how they are doing, they respond that they are just trying to keep their heads above water. New principals traditionally are hired in the summer months. At that time, they begin juggling balls immediately:

1. Creating a master schedule to accommodate course requests.
2. Interviewing and hiring teachers and staff.
3. Ensuring the building is ready for the upcoming school year to include cleanliness (cleaning schedules, locker combination resets, and so on), furniture needs, and technology needs and updates.
4. Ensuring materials are available to include textbooks, program equipment, teacher supplies, custodial supplies, and so on.
5. Planning multiple programs such as new teacher orientation, new student orientation, open house events, schedule pickups, locker rentals (if they have lockers), and so on.
6. Submit all state reports, and there are a slew of them.

The summer months are filled with managerial duties just to begin the school year. These are very important duties to fulfill and are very time consuming. Where in that time does a principal have time to analyze school achievement data, speak with teachers about instructional strengths and weaknesses of a school, develop a Leadership Team focused on data and instruction, research best practices, develop clear instructional goals with that Leadership Team, and develop a comprehensive professional development plan to address the goals? Again, these new principals start their first years trying to catch up.

Principal Preparation Programs

Some would argue that principal preparation programs are not doing enough to prepare first-year principals for the job they encounter (Bayar, 2016; Clock & Wells, 2015). Some view college professors as those who stand before students and tell war stories of years past. Certainly, this author cannot answer for all colleges and universities on this matter, but there is an alternate viewpoint to consider.

Principals are trained to become instructional leaders in their college preparation programs through courses like assessment of school programs and secondary curriculum development. Admittedly, these courses have not always existed in certification programs. However, most colleges and universities have partnerships with their neighboring districts to continuously evaluate and evolve their programs to fit the changing needs of the industry.

So, why are so many principals underprepared for the job at hand? The argument can be made that once these new principals get boots on the ground, they are so inundated with the managerial tasks of day-to-day operations that they don't think about the systems they need in place beforehand.

Additionally, think about this. When a teacher completes a master's program to gain administrative certification, that teacher will statistically remain in the teacher role for an average of five years (U.S. Department of Labor, 2019). Once that teacher gains an assistant principal role, that assistant principal is taught his/her responsibilities. That administrator will become proficient in his/her lane, not veering much from that lane because administrators often feel pressure to stay in their lane.

The average tenure of that assistant principal prior to obtaining a principalship is an estimated additional five years. At this point, the candidate is now ten years or more removed from the certification program. That individual became proficient in a lane, but all of a sudden, that individual is responsible for the entire highway system. Often, principal candidates are not prepared for that transition when they are given the keys to a building and are told to go forth and do well. Survival mode, again, kicks in pretty rapidly.

If these new principals put systems in place up front, all of the challenges would be more easily handled, and instructional leadership would not suffer. Through the principal struggle to keep up and put out fires, principals can become more reliant on others to provide that leadership, like a district office. This reality, unfortunately, occurs more frequently than it should. As a result, teachers and eventually students suffer.

SYSTEMS NEEDED

So, let's go back to the systems needed. To begin with systems, you must think systemically. What can be sustained through time? What systemic processes can be put in place to ensure that the important aspect of instructional leadership is not lost? What structures need to be in place to support the processes? Will the system operate in the principal's absence? A principal must think through these questions. Let's think about the structure for a minute. See figure 1.2.

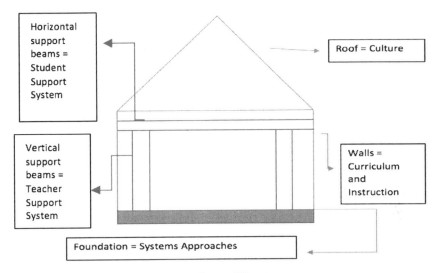

Figure 1.2   School Structure Compared to Building Structure.

Foundation

In order to have a system, you must understand the support structures needed. The comparison will be drawn to the structure of a schoolhouse. The systemic approach, or systems approach, provides the foundation for the entire schoolhouse. Whether the principal is thinking about instructional leadership or building maintenance, there must be a system in place for teachers and staff to employ in order to learn or to alert the principal of a building need.

What are these systems? They certainly can vary from building to building, but, nonetheless, they need to exist. Teachers need that structure to know what to expect and what is expected of them. Without this structure, it is like trying to hit a moving target. Efficiency and effectiveness are certainly lost, but frustration is also created. This is a sure-fire way to lose support in your building as a principal. So, the first element of a schoolhouse is the foundation or systems approach. The systems lens is the lens a principal must always look through in order to establish routines and process, answer questions, and create culture.

Instructional Support System

The second part of the schoolhouse structure is the walls themselves. Think of how a building is constructed. Foundation first, then exterior walls, or framing. The exterior walls are metaphorically the instructional leadership system. Some might argue that the walls should metaphorically be something else like a discipline management system, but this author will argue that instructional leadership is the primary concern for principals.

Think about classroom teachers for a minute. When teachers have classroom management issues, what element is most consistently missing? Bandura (1997) stated that teacher instructional self-efficacy, or the belief that they have control over achieving the goal, helping children learn, is vital to success in the classroom. Without this self-efficacy, principals are subject to burn out and ineffectiveness. However, this self-efficacy in instruction is the key, just like it is the key for classroom management and achievement (Skaalvik & Skaalvik, 2017).

Schools are all measured by how students achieve, aren't they? Classroom management issues most often relate to instructional strategies and teacher self-efficacy (McLeod, Fisher, & Hoover, 2003; Kameenui & Darch, 1995). So, it stands to reason that instructional leadership systems will impact behavior management systems as well, just like the classroom environment.

As stated earlier, educators live in a constant state of change, and this change also includes the state standards to be taught in each classroom. In SC alone, nearly every subject's standards have changes in the last three years. Some have changed more than once in that same time period.

As such, principals need to ensure that what is being taught in the classroom is aligned to those standards, assessments are cognitively aligned, and progress monitoring of data to adjust as needed is employed. This sounds simple, but it requires many moving parts to be effective. Sometimes, teachers need professional development in order to make the changes required of them.

Teacher Support System

Now, when thinking about constructing a house, what is the next step? First, the foundation is poured. Then, framing ensues with support beams. Yes, support structures are needed. These support structures constitute teacher support systems and student support systems. Teacher support beams are the vertical support beams because teachers help to "hold up" and support our students. Let's face it, teachers do the "work" of schools, and they should be appreciated for it. This teacher support system needs to include many areas:

1. Instructional Support
2. Professional Development
3. Evaluation Support
4. Human Support

Notice that human support is listed. Teachers need to be treated as individual humans who have lives outside of their jobs. This type of support can mean the most to teachers and reduce turnover rates. Shawnta Barnes (2017) pointed out that teachers do not quit their jobs, but they quit their bosses. Principals determine the culture of the school, whether it is sterile and uncaring or humanistic.

You can take a humanistic approach and still maintain your nonnegotiables. Teachers are happy with structure and guidance, but they want to know that you care. They are no different than students in that regard. Without proper teacher support, an administrator will never be successful.

Student Support System

Student supports are multilayered as well. Students today need more support than ever. The school has, and not just symbolically, become the hub of a community to provide support for families: emotional support, financial support at times, academic support, parenting support, legal support, and so on. No wonder students often come to school not ready to learn. Think about Maslow's Hierarchy of Needs in figure 1.3 (Maslow, 1970). The theory is that there is an order of needs that must be met in order for an individual to become self-actualized, or to become the best version of him/herself. If the first basic need, starting from the bottom, is not met, then the proceeding needs cannot be met. Think about your students when reviewing these needs.

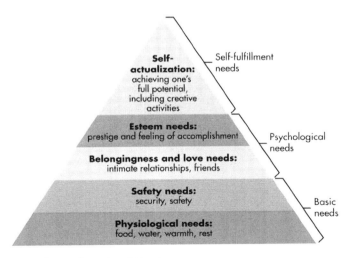

Figure 1.3 Maslow's Hierarchy of Needs.

Physiological Needs

Students often come to school hungry, tired, and feeling the elements of the weather. Those children that live in poverty are most susceptible to physiological needs not being met. The number of homelessness has grown in only twenty of the fifty states, but the number is still staggering. In January 2017, the national estimate of homelessness in America is over half a million people, with over 400,000 identified as households (Council of Economic Advisors, 2019).

Think about the number of children that are affected. This number does not include the number of families that reside with other family or friends due to poverty. That number exceeded 4.5 million in 2016, up 30 percent since 2007 (Council of Economic Advisors, 2019). Basic physiological needs are not being met for many of our children today. Schools are still charged with educating these students who essentially are not prepared to learn. So, what is the school's response? Schools often set up food and clothing banks for their communities to help feed and clothe the neediest of their populations. If parents feel that they can come to their school administration for support when needed, they will. However, trust must be established first. Lisbeth and Daniel Schorr's (1998) research on working with the disadvantaged showed that social assistance works best when administered by someone who is known and trusted. Who better to trust than your school's principal? Warren, Thompson, and Saegert (2001) stated simply, "We need to look at norms of cooperation and trust not as a general resource, but as they affect what people actually do—for our concerns, the processes of community building and collective action" (p. 8).

Trusting relationships must be established with your needy community so that a school can serve as a support and connection to the outside agencies who can offer further assistance. In essence, schools help to build community. Often, the solution for some lies in access to resources, and the most impoverished just need some assistance in making those connections. However, if those in need are not comfortable asking and those in power are not astute enough or are not attentive enough to understand the dilemma, the situation will never change.

SAFETY NEEDS

To think that our children are not safe is an unwelcome thought, but the fact remains that many of our students reside in homes or situations that are not safe from drugs and violence. A 2009 Department of Justice Study showed that more than 60 percent of children surveyed were exposed to violence, either directly or indirectly as a victim or witness. The long-term effects of such violence can lead to troubles in school, emotional issues, drug and/ or alcohol abuse, and possibly even criminal activities (Finkelhor, Turner, Omrod, Hamby & Kracke, 2009).

These children need to have a support system in school that not only affords an outlet but also works to protect and defend. Children need to see adults as protectors, even if the protection is needed from the parent. How can these children possibly come to school ready to learn? Administrators, teachers, counselors, and so on need to establish trust with their students so that students will feel comfortable sharing any unsafe situations. All school personnel need to be trained to recognize the signs and understand the system of response and support.

Safety needs also include safety to and from school as well as while in school. Many children live in neighborhoods that do not evoke feelings of safety, and crime statistics are on the rise. Just watch the evening news; it is quite depressing. How do children process all of the craziness that surrounds them? When one types in "children and neighborhood safety" on Google, there are nearly eleven million hits. If adults are not having real conversations with children about how to avoid unsafe situations, they are doing them a true disservice.

A principal must convey the message to parents and teachers that the number one priority is safety. That edict should include safe travels to and from school, which a principal can help influence with bus routes, talks with local law enforcement, and so on. Adults also need to discuss what is actually happening in the world rather than allowing children to hear some pundit with a political agenda. According to the American Academy of Child and Adolescent Psychiatry (2019), children can develop stress, fear, and anxiety based on reporting of world events. This media influence must not be ignored. Real discussions need to occur in school and at home in order for children to understand the world in which they live and help them remain safe.

SOCIAL NEEDS

Students, just like adults, need to feel a sense of belonging and friendship. Schools need to have systems in place, whether through small groups or with extracurricular activities, that support all students. According to Osterman (2010),

> When students experience belonging in the school community, their needs for relatedness are met in ways that affect their attitudes and their behavior. They like school and are more engaged in learning. They have more positive attitudes toward themselves and others and are more likely to interact with others—peers

and adults, in positive and supportive ways. They are more accepting and more empathetic to others. Conversely, the sense of rejection is associated with emotional distress as well as a full range of behavioral, social, and academic problems. (p. 239)

This sense of belonging not only has to exist in the school as a whole but also inside each classroom. Teachers have to foster this development with a nurturing environment and instructional strategies that fit the needs of the students. Students who feel a sense of belonging will also develop a sense of pride in their school. A recent study by the National Federation of State High School Associations shows that students who have school spirit will perform better academically (2015). Students who feel they belong and have friends are most assuredly more apt to have school spirit. Administrators can make concerted efforts to ensure that all students have a place to belong in the school.

Esteem Needs

Every person needs to feel a sense of accomplishment and worth, and students are no different. Self-esteem not only encapsulates a sense of self-worth but also a sense of self-control (Ross & Broh, 2000). Students can not only feel good about themselves but also feel they have no control over their choices and subsequent futures. This conflict needs to be resolved through conversation, resource alignment, and trust. In doing so, students then can work toward an achievable goal, which will improve academic performance.

A system of rewards also needs to be in place to recognize and reward accomplishment, achievement, and improvement. A large number of students just want to know that someone cares enough to pay attention, to be honest. These systems need to be multilayered: in the classroom, in school activities, in community events, in publications, in the school as a whole. Each layer serves to support the sense of accomplishment of the individual and of the school, bolstering more school and community pride as well as school spirit. In essence, a system needs to be in place to make the school the biggest cheerleader for students. Sounds simple, but it is very powerful.

Self-Actualization

In order to achieve one's full potential while in school, the eye always needs to be on the prize. Students need to receive and believe the message that they will graduate, even if they have to be dragged across the stage, kicking and screaming. However, the focus should be on planning for what comes after high school. Spending time focused on next steps is imperative so that all students know the future they want is a possibility.

Parents have to understand that their jobs are to make sure that any and every choice for what their children want to be when they grow up, from ditch digger to brain surgeon, is an actual choice. Parents should help develop and support their children to get them both to that point of selection; then, it is up to the students to walk through those doors and take control. Our students deserve the same in schools. This system entails one of academic support, career planning, connection to resources, and so on. If students believe they can achieve the goal, they will work harder for it.

CULTURE SYSTEM

Culture, as said in the south, is "how we do things around here." By definition, culture would then relate to systems, processes, and procedures. However, culture is so much more than the mechanics of a system. Culture is tangible. Parents and community members will say that a school has a feeling about it, warm and inviting with happy people everywhere. Culture is not an accident of nature; it is created. Creating culture is time consuming but oh so powerful. Peterson and Deal (1998) describe a positive school culture as one in which the following exists:

- where staff have a shared sense of purpose, where they pour their hearts into teaching;
- where the underlying norms are of collegiality, improvement, and hard work;
- where student rituals and traditions celebrate student accomplishment, teacher innovation, and parental commitment;
- where the informal network of storytellers, heroes, and heroines provides a social web of information, support, and history;
- where success, joy, and humor abound. (p. 29)

Think about how you create each of these aspects of a positive school culture. Many school leaders allow culture to evolve naturally, but this author warns that this is a huge misstep. One must define the culture you want to create, and then set about actually creating it. If you ignore culture, all other aspects of schooling, including academic achievement, will suffer.

SYSTEMS PERSPECTIVE

Principals must understand the systems that are needed in their schools to first establish a system. Administrators should take stock of what elements of each system exist and what elements are missing—what would they like to see in the curriculum and instructional system or in the culture system? Elements for each system exist in schools, but they may not be systemically planned.

SUMMARY

This chapter has briefly discussed four major systems that principals need to establish, manage, and lead in order to maximize a school's impact on its students, teachers, and community:

1. Curriculum and Instruction System
2. Teacher Support System
3. Student Support System
4. Culture System

Each chapter of this book will break down the first two systems and their component parts and describe how to establish the systems needed. Of course, one must realize that this is a process that does not happen overnight. Change is difficult for people, inherently. However, this book will discuss how to initiate this change over time, in a nonthreatening manner. Additionally, this book serves to create an awareness of the multiple systems that need to operate simultaneously.

There is no right way or wrong way to establish these systems. Of course, one must do what is best for the school, and each school community is different. Nonetheless, each of these systems must be developed in every school. Understanding the multilayers of school administration is half the battle. Ready to begin?

A PIECE AT A TIME

- What lens should a principal use when developing programs in schools?
- What are the four basic systems needed in schools?
- What are the elements of a strong instructional system?
- In a teacher support system, what are the four factors to consider?
- What factors should be considered when developing a student support system?
- What are some of the elements of positive school culture?
- Where systems or elements of systems exist within your school?
- What elements are missing in your school?

REFERENCES

Aacap. (2019, January). News and children. Retrieved March 13, 2019, from https://www.aacap.org/aacap/families_and_youth/facts_for_families/fff-guide/Children-And-The-News-067.aspx.

Bandura, A. (1997). *Self-efficacy: The exercise of control.* New York: W.H. Freeman and Company.

Batanen, B., Grissom, J. & Rogers, L. (2019). The impacts of principal turnover. *Educational Evaluation and Policy Analysis, 41*(3), 350–74.

Bayar, A. (2016). Challenges facing principals in the first year at their schools. *Universal Journal of Educational Research, 4*(1), 192–99.

Board Member Selection and Meetings [PDF]. (2017, October). Columbia: South Carolina School Board's Association.

Clock, B. A. & Wells, C. M. (2015). Workload pressures of principals: A focus on Renewal, support, and mindfulness. *NASSP Bulletin, 99*(4), 332–55.

Council of Economic Advisors. (2019). The state of homelessness in America. Washington, DC.

Finkelhor, D., Turner, H., Omrod, R., Hamby, S., & Kracke, K. (2009, October). Juvenile Justice Bulletin (United States, U. S. Department of Justice, Justice Programs). Retrieved March 13, 2019, from http://www.ncjrs.gov/pdffiles1/ojjdp/227 7-44.pdf.

Fuller, E. (2012). Examining principal turnover. Retrieved March 1, 2019, from http://nepc.colorado.edu/blog/examining-principal-turnover.

Granata, K. (2019, February 14). Report looks at high cost and rate of principal turnover. Retrieved March 1, 2019, from https://www.educationworld.com/a_news/report-looks-high-cost-and-rate-principal-turnover-1980898737.

Kameenui, E. J. & Darch, C. B. (1995). *Instructional classroom management: A proactive approach to behavior management.* White Plains, NY: Longman.

Mark, W. R., Thompson, P., & Seagert, S. (2001). Chapter 1: The role of social capital in combating poverty. In: Susan Seagart, J. Phillip Thompson and Mark Warren (eds.). *Social capital and poor communities* (pp. 1–28). New York, NY: Russel Sage Foundation.

Maslow, A. H. (1970). *Motivation and personality* (2nd ed.). New York: Harper and Row.

McLeod, S. (2018). Maslow's hierarchy of needs. *Simply Psychology.* Retrieved March 13, 2019, from https://www.simplypsychology.org/maslow.html.

McLeod, J., Fisher, J., & Hoover, G. (2003). *The key elements of classroom management: Managing time and space, student behavior, and instructional strategies.* Alexandria, Virginia: ASCD.

Osterman, K. F. (2000). Students' need for belonging in the school community. *Review of Educational Research, 70,* 323–67.

Peterson, K. & Deal, T. (1998). Realizing a positive school climate: How leaders Influence the culture of schools. *Educational Leadership, 56*(1), 28–30.

Riddell, R. (2018, May 9). Report: Average superintendent tenure about 6 years (Issue brief). Retrieved March 12, 2019, from Education Dive website: https://ww

w.educationdive.com/news/report-average-superintendent-tenure-about-6-years/523089/.

Ross, C. & Broh, B. (2000). The roles of self-esteem and the sense of personal control in the academic achievement process. *Sociology of Education, 73*(4), 270–84.

Schorr, L. B. & Schorr, D. (1989). *Within our reach: Breaking the cycle of disadvantage.* New York: Doubleday.

Skaalvik, E. M. & Skaalvik, S. (2017). Teacher stress and teacher self-efficacy: Relations and consequences. In: McIntyre T., McIntyre S., and Francis D. (eds.). *Educator Stress. Aligning Perspectives on Health, Safety and Well-Being.* New York, NY: Springer.

South Carolina Legislature Online. (n.d.). Retrieved March 13, 2019, from http://www.scstatehouse.gov/.

State of Homelessness (Rep.). (2019). Retrieved March 13, 2019, from National Alliance to End Homelessness website: https://endhomelessness.org/homelessness-in-america/homelessness-statistics/state-of-homelessness-report/.

Survey Shows Students with School Spirit are Top Achievers. (2015, February 5). Retrieved March 13, 2019, from https://www.nfhs.org/articles/survey-shows-students-with-school-spirit-are-top-achiever.

Tyre, P. (2015, September 26). Why do more than half of principals quit after 5 years? (Rep.). Retrieved March 1, 2019, from Hechinger Report website: https://hechingerreport.org/why-do-more-than-half-of-principals-quit-after-five-years/.

United States Department of Labor. (2019). Elementary, middle and high school principals. Occupational Outlook Handbook. Washington, DC.

Part I

A SYSTEM OF CURRICULUM AND INSTRUCTION

A system of curriculum and instruction is a basic necessity for schools to be successful. Without one, teachers have no direction on what to teach and whether or not they are truly preparing their students. This system should include the issues of curricular alignment, assessments, curriculum maps, lesson plans, lesson plan critiques, observations, and feedback. This system should drive the work of teaching and learning, and administrators need to lead this charge.

Chapter 2

Curriculum Alignment

Design is not just what it looks like and feels like. Design is how it works.

—*Steve Jobs*

The analogy of building a house will continue to be used throughout this text. So, the first chapter provided the foundation: looking through a systems lens. This chapter then focuses on the next step in constructing that house—framing the outer walls. The outer walls of a structure give the structure its shape—its purpose. Schools provide many services for students and a community, but its primary focus is an institution of learning; therefore, it makes sense that the outer walls of our schoolhouse are comprised of a system of curriculum and instruction.

A school's system of curriculum and instruction is the basis of a successful school and must be developed and refined along with a system of instructional supervision. In clarifying this system, teachers can answer the following questions with some ease:

1. What am I supposed to teach?
2. How much time do I have to teach each standard?
3. In what curriculum are my state standards being addressed?
4. At what cognitive level should I teach the standards?
5. What resources are available to help me teach these standards?
6. How do I assess student learning of these standards?
7. What strategies do I employ?
8. How do I respond when students need enrichment?
9. How do I respond when students do not learn?
10. How do I meet the instructional expectations of my administration?

The first five questions will be addressed in this chapter and the remaining questions in the subsequent chapters.

When teachers know what is expected of them and are provided with guidance and resources, they can operate without fear. Most teachers' specific asset to a school is their content knowledge (Hoy, Davis, & Pape, 2006). Teachers pride themselves on knowing their subject matter, and they should as they are experts in their fields!

However, teachers do not always feel confident in their teaching, which is separate from their content knowledge (Lewis, 2009; Tygret, 2018). Prior to the advent of state standards, teachers always worried if they were teaching what kids needed to be successful.

Consequently, a strong curriculum allows teachers to feel confident that what they are teaching is essential and required (Boudah, Lenz, Schumaker, & Deshler, 2008). This strong curriculum and instruction program encompasses many elements: curriculum, assessments, instructional strategies, resources, remediation, and enrichment opportunities (Ainsworth, 2014). Each element must work together in order to inform one another.

This multifaceted system must have strong roots and support in order for students and teachers to feel successful. So, how does one create a system for curriculum and instruction? How does a principal know that the system is operating effectively? One must begin with the basic fundamental component of curriculum alignment.

CURRICULUM ALIGNMENT

Most districts have a curriculum guide that informs teachers what they must teach. This is the basic, rudimentary necessity of an instructional program. Teachers can remember teaching when standards were in draft form, and teachers were given a textbook and a classroom. Times have certainly changed! Consequently, most districts have expanded the curriculum guides to include rich curriculum development that shows the alignment of the material to the state standards.

With the advent of standards, teachers have to figure out in what content they will teach the standards. English teachers, specifically, have the task of determining in which pieces of literature they will teach the standards. Heidi Hayes Jacobs paved the way with curriculum mapping. Jacobs (1996) and Squires (2012) explained that one must map out the standards in the content to be taught to ensure that all standards were taught.

Seems like a simple concept, but it was and is still not simple for many. So many teachers became reliant on textbooks in which publishers claimed that the texts were aligned to the standards. Teachers did not have to think about the sequence and outcomes, the textbook provided that information. The problem is that these same textbooks were and continue to be sold across the country, and not all states share the same standards. Also, textbooks are intended to be a resource, not the curriculum itself.

Mapping

Once the standards are in context of the instructional materials, mapping should be taken a step further, and teachers must dive into the alignment of the cognitive level of the standard. This type of mapping requires a much more in-depth analysis of what the standards are asking, and this is crucial work. Well-developed curriculum maps or unit organizers include the unwrapped standards: the concepts students need to know, the skills they need to be able to do, the cognitive demand, the teaching targets, and required resources (Ainsworth, 2014; Jacobs, 1996).

If the district's curriculum map does not include all of these elements, then work can be done with teachers to understand and develop these concepts. In order to do so, one must truly understand Bloom's Taxonomy, Webb's Depth of Knowledge (DOK), and how the two intersect.

Most educators have heard of and worked with Bloom's Taxonomy on multiple occasions. This hierarchy of cognitive skills was revised by Anderson and Krathwohl (2001) to include cognitive processes, such as the following: understand, apply, synthesize, evaluate, and create. These same cognitive processes can be found in state standards today.

As such, it is imperative that the curriculum must be mapped and aligned to the new cognitive processes rather than the old cognitive skills of knowledge, comprehension, application, and so on. This change should be reflected in the unit organizers to show what students are to be able to do as well as the cognitive demand of the standards. Ainsworth (2014) stated that teachers need a rigorous curriculum in which all elements are intentionally aligned to the standards in order to guide instruction effectively.

Let's look at the example in figure 2.1 in what we will call a beginning curriculum map. This map only begins to give the necessary components in a quality curriculum for teachers. The state standards are listed first, and then the following breakdown provides the skills and what the students should actually do as a result of learning the standard. Maps are most helpful when they break down what the students need to know, the skills required, and how that translates to student action.

Required resources should be included so that teachers know in what materials they are teaching particular standards with some supplemental

EII-RL.5.1/EII-RI.5.1 Cite strong and thorough textual evidence to support analysis of what the text says explicitly as well as inferences drawn from the text; identify multiple supported interpretations.		
Need to Know	Skills	What it Means
Evidence	Cite	cite evidence
Inference	Identify	
EII-RL.12.2 Analyze how an author's choices concerning how to structure a text, order events within the text, and manipulate time to create different effects.		
Events Within the Text Manipulation of Time & Text Structure	Analyze	determine significance of text structure and manipulation of time

Figure 2.1   Beginning Curriculum Map.

resources. Without these fundamental pieces, there will be no continuity in learning in and among classrooms. This guidance allows teachers to effectively plan ahead and prepare.

Now, these requirements do not tell teachers how to teach the material to students, which still allows teachers flexibility with their craft. Teachers can also use supplemental resources to take a deeper dive into the standards. However, this consistency with required materials among teachers allows administrators to progress monitor, which will be talked about more later in this chapter.

Let's look at figure 2.2 for a slightly revised curriculum map. By adding the concepts to be taught and the required resources, teachers know exactly

EII-RL.5.1/EII-RI.5.1 Cite strong and thorough textual evidence to support analysis of what the text says explicitly as well as inferences drawn from the text; identify multiple supported interpretations.			
Need to Know	Skills	What It Means	Required Resources
Evidence	Cite	Cite Evidence	A Shakespeare play such as *The Taming of the Shrew, Much Ado About Nothing, The Merchant of Venice or The Tragedy of Julius Caesar*
Inference	Identify		
EII-RL.12.2 Analyze how an author's choices concerning how to structure a text, order events within the text, and manipulate time to create different effects.			
Events Within the Text Manipulation of Time & Text Structure	Analyze	determine significance of text structure and manipulation of time	Same as above or *Twelve Angry Men* by Reginald Rose

Figure 2.2   Slightly Revised Curriculum Map.

what materials, what standards, what skills and concepts they are teaching in the unit. This map takes most of the guesswork out of teaching by narrowing the curricular focus (King & Zucker, 2005). By providing the concepts, teachers should know what instructional elements they will use to teach the standards, but they can also be specified.

To improve this map, additional resources should be provided for teachers and instructional elements, and in doing so, a complete picture can be provided for teachers. Granted, this map only represents two standards. To truly be complete, each standard with each supporting standard would have to be included in the map, along with each element provided for each supporting standard (see figure 2.3).

EII-RL.5.1/EII-RI.5.1 Cite strong and thorough textual evidence to support analysis of what the text says explicitly as well as inferences drawn from the text; identify multiple supported interpretations.				Additional Resources
Need to Know	Skills	What It Means	Required Resources	
Evidence Inference	Cite Identify	Cite Evidence	A Shakespeare play such as *The Taming of the Shrew, Much Ado About Nothing, The Merchant of Venice* or *The Tragedy of Julius Caesar*	Close reading with JC https://www.folger.edu/close-reading-the-conspiracy-in-act-2 Folger' Library www.folger.edu http://www.shakespeare-online.com https://www.tes.com/teaching-shakespeare/themes/
EII-RL.12.2 Analyze how an author's choices concerning how to structure a text, order events within the text, and manipulate time to create different effects.				
Events Within the Text Manipulation of Time & Text Structure	Analyze	determine significance of text structure and manipulation of time	Same as above or *Twelve Angry Men* by Reginald Rose	https://www.prestwickhouse.com/blog/post/2017/12/how-to-teach-twelve-angry-men http://www.samandscout.com/drama-and-persuasion-mini-unit-with-twelve-angry-men/ https://edsitement.neh.gov/launchpad-activities-twelve-angry-men
Concepts: Central idea, claim, counterclaim, rebuttal, evidence, false statements, reasoning				
Required Instructional Elements: Writing, Research, Close Reading				

Figure 2.3   Complete Instructional Map.

The process of completing instructional mapping is very time consuming; however, the end result is one of the best supports for teachers since the advent of textbooks. Textbooks are intended to be utilized as resources, not the curriculum itself (Ball & Cohen, 1996; Boote, 2006). With the addition of so many online resources, a teacher could get lost in the jungle of information without a solid guide. If your district's curriculum maps do not integrate all of these elements, it is time to convene groups of experts, your teachers, to help complete the maps.

Systems Perspective

As an administrator, you should look at a curriculum alignment system as your first step in instructional leadership. Certainly, you are not expected to be an expert in all content areas, for this would be almost impossible. However, you can ensure that this fundamental basis of instruction is in place and utilized with fidelity in your school.

To begin this step, you have to think about your school staff and infrastructure.

1. What personnel do you have?
2. What are their strengths?
3. How is the curriculum map accessible to teachers?
4. What time do teachers have to work with the maps?

In assessing your staff and their strengths, you can build a system that aides you in this endeavor. For example, when hiring assistant principals, a principal should try to ensure that the administrative team contains a diverse representation of curricular areas: math, science, English, social studies, and so on. This allows a principal to share the responsibility of the system with curricular experts. If your team is not well-rounded, you can also look at your teacher leaders.

Some districts allow department chairs additional planning time to perform the duties of the department chair. If this is the case, certainly, these professionals should be part of the system. However, they are never to work in isolation. All personnel who engage in the system need to report to the principal. The principal must always be seen as the instructional leader in the school.

Below are some examples (figures 2.4 and 2.5) of the system structure. You can adapt and change people and positions based on your school's makeup. It is important to notice that all players are equal. Information is shared with and among each person, but the principal is in the thick of it, rolling up his or her sleeves to engage in the work. Principals cannot do the job alone, and it is folly to think otherwise.

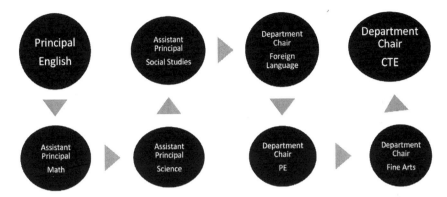

Figure 2.4   Instructional Team 1.

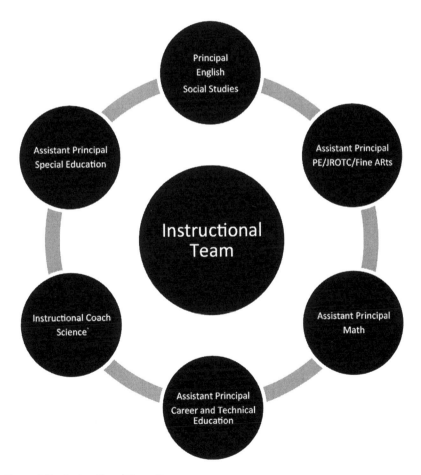

Figure 2.5   Instructional Team 2.

The above is a simple structure used in schools where departmental chairs are not afforded any additional planning time, and the principal does not wish to overburden them. Notice, the principal undertook the largest two departments, setting the stage for others. Principals must always model the behavior expected.

Your team is in place, now what? If your district's curriculum map includes all of the necessary elements, you move right to progress monitoring. If not, you start working with the departments to add the missing elements to the existing maps. You also need to understand how the maps are accessible for teachers. Are they online? Are they fixed, meaning, can text be added to them if there are missing pieces and parts? If not, you may want to create your own within your building. Software that allows sharing is best, like OneNote or Google.

Remember that developing these maps is hard work and will take time. Changes made in education should be considered in a process design. Nothing is instantaneous. However, the process of developing the maps will affect instruction in your building immediately. Teachers will start to think about their materials more closely and purposefully.

The time needed for the work to add to maps is a critical component. Teachers are already inundated and overwhelmed with the increasing responsibility and rigor. So, if possible, find a way to compensate them for their efforts. Working after school and in the summer is infringing on their time, and they would appreciate compensation, for sure. In states with unions, this would be required. The time and money will be resources well spent.

Now that the system is in place, it is time to progress monitor the curriculum alignment. The system for curriculum alignment will look like what is represented in figure 2.6 if your district does not have a rich curriculum aligned to the standards.

PROGRESS MONITORING FOR ADMINISTRATORS

With a comprehensive curriculum map which includes all elements (standards, skills, resources and instructional elements) like that depicted in figure 2.3, administrators can progress monitor the curriculum alignment in their building of lesson plans. Think about this for a minute. Lesson plans can tell you a myriad of things: if teachers are on pace with the curriculum map, if they are adhering to the map, strategies teachers may employ, and what observations should reveal in the classroom. All of this information is important for an administrator to know in real time, as progress monitoring is a tool of effective leadership (Harris et al., 2017).

If a teacher is struggling with pacing, you may not be made aware until the state assessments are administered and results are published, and everyone

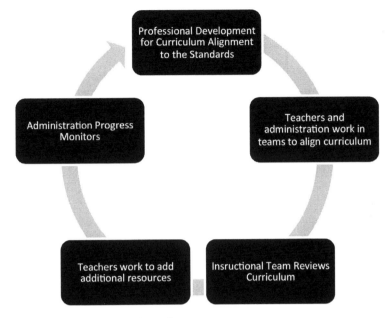

Figure 2.6   System for Curriculum Alignment.

knows that is too late. What if a teacher is not following the curriculum map because she has a passion for creative writing? You, unfortunately, probably will not know until you get a call from your superintendent about test scores in your school.

In essence, decisions cannot be made about teacher support, professional development, resources needed, and so on without knowing what is happening instructionally in your building. Lesson plans not only provide an instructional map for teachers but also a roadmap of learning for administrators. The importance of lesson plans cannot be understated, as reflective teachers analyze their plans and their effectiveness (Zhukova, 2018).

Furthermore, observations should be aligned to lesson plans. Sounds like a simple statement that should be obvious. However, sometimes teachers may stray from plans and never fully teach the standards. An administrator would never know otherwise without the lesson plan review coupled with focused observations.

Admittedly, a number of school administrators have teachers turn in their lesson plans, but for what purpose? Teachers should not have to spend time creating something that is never read; teachers have to trust that principals value their work (Tschannen-Moran & Gareis, 2015; Bellibas & Liu, 2017).

If teachers know that you are not reviewing lesson plans, they may not put the whole effort you want into them. Why should they? A survey of

administrators about their procedures for lesson plans revealed responses that
are wide and varied:

1. Teachers are not required to turn them in.
2. Teachers turn them into their department heads.
3. Teachers post them on the outside of their rooms or must have them
    available when being observed.
4. Teachers submit them to the administration for random spot checks.
5. Teachers turn them into administration but administration does not have
    time to read them.
6. Teachers turn them in to the administration for review.

Your school policy on lesson plans sets the stage for the instructional
program in your school (Shen, Poppink, Cui, & Fan, 2007). If they are not
required, then you are sending the message to your teachers that planning
is not important. Remember, where teachers see you spend your time as an
administrator is what they see you value as an administrator. If you do not
spend a fair amount of time on curriculum and instruction in your school, and
instead spend the majority of the time on buses, butts, books, and putting out
fires, that is what teachers think you value.

Despite what you may tell them your vision is for the school, that is not
what you are communicating through action. Leithwood, Day, Sammons,
Hopkins, and Harris (2006) studied effective school leadership practices,
and it is no wonder that leading the instructional program is among the most
important practices of effective school leaders. Therefore, it stands to reason
that if you want teachers to spend time thoughtfully creating their lessons
to engage students at the cognitive level of the standard, then lesson plans
should be valued.

One principal required lesson plans to be posted outside of each classroom
door so that an observer could review then prior to walking into a classroom
and would know what he or she was witnessing. On an instructional walk
with his supervisor, that principal found that the posted lesson plans were all
outdated and/or incomplete. In fact, one teacher's lesson plans were from two
months prior. This fact revealed a couple of things to the principal.

No one was looking at lesson plans. No one was using them prior to
observations, and/or no one was observing instruction. Additionally, the
teacher did not value planning because the administration did not value it.
This administrator did not have knowledge about what was occurring in
the classrooms. This is not the message a principal wants to send to his/her
supervisor.

Granted, depending on the size of the school, lesson plan review can be
quite cumbersome. Therefore, you need to develop a system that works for

your school size. Here is a list of things to consider when setting your lesson plan process:

1. Due Date and Time
   a. Do you want teachers to turn in their lesson plans in advance of the teaching period?
   b. What time of day do you want them submitted? If you don't specify, you may be receiving lesson plans up until midnight of that day.
2. Attachments
   a. Are the week's formative assessments attached?
   b. Are rubrics, performance tasks, or summative assessments also attached?
3. Reviewers
   a. Who will review the lesson plans?
   b. How will teachers receive feedback?
   c. What timeframe is given for review?

It is important to have assessments attached to lesson plans, and this will be discussed in the next chapter. Certainly, assessments need to be considered in your lesson plan process. Admittedly, teachers need to understand the importance of the work you are asking of them, and administrators need to inspect what they expect, consistently (Clinton, 2009).

Think of the system like the one in table 2.1. The principal assuming the responsibility of two large departments lets the teachers know that the principal is serious about instructions. Leaving comments in regard to suggestions, questions, and praises tell the teachers that the principal not only reads plans closely but is also vested.

In leaving suggestions, teachers view administration as a resource, which is invaluable (Blasé, 2000). Open conversations can occur about instructional strategies and resources; in turn, teachers are motivated to invite administrators to observe a class and participate in fun learning projects in addition to asking for assistance in solving problems and brainstorming ideas. For example, imagine the following situation:

A math teacher is having difficulty with students grasping simple geometry concepts at the beginning of the course. She explains to the principal that if she were applying geometry to real-world situations, students do not have a basis of understanding: when discussing a ladder leaning against a wall, students could not understand that a triangle was formed. So, the principal and teacher brainstormed for a few minutes, and the principal suggested teaching a construction in geometry unit. The plan is to have the math teacher work in conjunction with the drama teacher to help build the set for the spring musical. Some hands-on experiences will allow students to understand the basic concepts moving forward in the course. The teacher is excited to try the new project, and see if it works well for the students.

This open dialogue was created through lesson plan review and subsequent conversations. The teacher truly views the principal as a resource, and the brainstorming provided for more engaging lessons for students. Priceless.

Some schools have lesson plan software programs. Of course, a program that houses all plans is preferential. However, simple emails also work. An administrator just has to remember to track who has turned them in each week by using a simple checklist of departmental staff. In doing so, an administrator is able to quickly email a teacher to request a tardy lesson plan as a "friendly reminder." The system, like in table 2.1, is easy to use and time consuming for administrators, but the benefits are vital to an instructional program.

As for the other members of the instructional team (IT), it is important to discuss what everyone is seeing in the lesson plans. Your team needs to know that you are interested and are monitoring their work as well. Administrators can make this part of their Monday morning meetings to discuss lesson plan review and observation data. As such, administrators will have a good feeling as to what is happening in all classrooms in the building.

Observation schedules can be built based on lesson plan reviews. Imagine that! In lesson plan discussion, each team member should be responsible to answer questions about pacing, materials, and instructional strategies, as well as assessments. More about assessments and strategies will come later; however, knowing about alignment, pacing, and materials is important, too, for several reasons.

For one, you can easily identify teachers who may need additional support and provide that support in a timely manner. In doing so, students can learn what is required of them. If the students' skills are deficient, then you can discuss with the teachers what elements of the map meet priority status.

Table 2.1   Sample Lesson Plan System

Lesson Plan System	Deadlines
Due Date	Fridays, the week prior to the week's lesson
Time	Due by 5:00 p.m.
Submission	Via Email
Review	Review by Sunday evening at 8:00 p.m.
Reviewer	Assigned Administration
English	Principal
Math	Instructional Coach
Science	Designated AP
Social Studies	Principal
PE/JROTC/Fine Arts	Designated AP
Career and Technical	Designated AP

AP Advanced Placement.

Sometimes, hard conversations have to be held. Additionally, you will know if a teacher is using materials that may be questioned later.

Imagine being questioned by parents or district office staff about controversial materials being taught and used within your school. You need to be informed and be part of the decision-making process about instructional materials. After all, you will be the one questioned about it and held accountable both publicly and privately. Knowing what is happening in your classrooms is also a way to protect yourself and your teachers.

A SYSTEMS PERSPECTIVE

Principals need to understand that a strong curriculum and instructional system is the foundation for learning in a school. There is absolutely no greater impact on student achievement than quality teaching. Therefore, teachers need guidance to ensure that all teachers are singing the same tune. This only occurs with a curriculum map. If this map does not exist in your district, it is up to you and your teachers to create one for your school. This map should include standards, materials, and resources. Developing a curriculum map is a huge undertaking.

Once the map is established, administrators need to monitor curriculum and instruction in their buildings through lesson plan review and comments. See figure 2.7 for a sample lesson plan critique. Weekly review of lesson plans will provide valuable information on the alignment of instruction as well as assessments. Discussions should follow with the administrative team about the patterns of behavior found in the building, either as strengths or weaknesses. This information will inform professional development needs.

Coupling lesson plan review with scheduled observations is crucial to understanding the alignment of instructional strategies in the building. Just as data is collected on lesson plans, data should be collected on observations as well. This information also informs professional development needs in the building. A system of review and feedback is imperative as a basis of a strong instructional program.

SUMMARY

Curriculum is the basis of the instructional system. Curriculum maps and unit organizers guide teachers on what to teach, not how to teach; so, teachers still have flexibility in their classrooms. Curriculum guides and unit organizers should contain the unwrapped standards, the concepts students need to know, the skills they need to be able to do, the cognitive demand of the standards, the DOK demands of the teaching targets, required resources, and supplemental resources.

A principal must establish the system for curriculum alignment, especially if the district's maps are not inclusive of all needed elements. The IT can take many different shapes, but it is important that the principal is an equal player on the team. Administrators must progress monitor this system through lesson plan review, and the review process must be established up front. Lesson plan review helps keep administrators informed about what is happening in their buildings.

Dimensions:	Mon	Tues	Wed	Thurs	Fri	Rating
1. Does the Lesson Plan (LP) include the **Content Standard(s)** appropriately for grade level? Include full standard.						
2. Does the Lesson Plan contain the **Essential Question(s)** aligned with the Content Standards?						
3. Does the Lesson Plan contain objectives written as "I Can" statements?						
4. The teacher has included **Technology** into the Lesson Plan for implementation during the lesson?						
5. Does the Lesson Plan contain **Direct Instruction** to demonstrate and model the content taught?						
6. Does the Lesson Plan contain **Guided Practice** to adequately identify what the learner will do?						
7. Does the Lesson Plan contain **Independent Practice** to adequately identify what the learner will do?						
8. Does the Lesson Plan components address **differences in students' learning**? (Ex. Rates, modalities, etc.) (adaptations/ differentiations)						
9. Does the Lesson Plan include a review of the standard taught and what the learner mastered?						
10. Does the Lesson Plan include attached **Assessments** for the week?						
11. Teacher has included appropriate						

Figure 2.7   Sample Lesson Plan Critique.

A PIECE AT A TIME

Consider the following after reading this chapter:

- Does your district provide a thorough curriculum map for teachers?
- What elements are included in your curriculum maps?
- How do you monitor curriculum alignment as an administrator?
- Do you read and comment on lesson plans? If so, what do you look for in the plans?
- What are the instructional expectations in your school? How do you monitor and support teachers with the expectations?

REFERENCES

Ainsworth, L. (2014). *Rigorous curriculum design: How to create curricular units of study that Align standards, instruction, and assessment.* Englewood, CO: The Leadership and Learning Center.

Anderson, L. W. & Krathwohl, D. R. (2001). *A taxonomy for learning, teaching, and assessing: A revision of bloom's taxonomy of educational objectives.* Boston, MA: Pearson Education Group.

Ball, D. & Cohen, D. (1996). Reform by the book: What is—or might be—the role of curriculum materials in teacher learning and instructional reform? *Educational Researcher, 25*(9), 6–8, 14.

Bellibas, M. & Liu, Y. (2017). Multilevel analysis of the relationship between principal's perceived practices of instructional leadership and teachers' self-efficacy perceptions. *Journal of Educational Administration, 55*(1), 49–69.

Black, P. & William, D. (1998). Assessment and classroom learning. *Educational Assessment: Principles, Policy & Practice, 5*(1), 7–74.

Black, P. & William, D. (2009). Developing the theory of formative assessment. *Educational Assessment, Evaluation and Accountability, 1*(1), 5–31.

Blasé, J. (2000). Effective instructional leadership: Teachers' perspectives on how principals promote teaching and learning in schools. *Journal of Educational Administration, 38*(2), 130–41.

Boote, D. (2006). Teachers' professional discretion and the curricula. *Teachers and Teaching Theory and Practice, 12*(4), 461–78.

Boudah, D., Lenz, K., Schumaker, J., & Deshler, D. (2008). Teaching in the face of academic diversity: Unit planning and instruction by secondary teachers to enhance learning in inclusive classes. *Journal of Curriculum and Instruction, 2*(2), 74–91.

Broadfoot, P. & Black, P. (2004). Redefining assessment? The first ten years of assessment in education. *Assessment in Education: Principles, Policy & Practice, 11*(1), 7–26.

Brookhart, S. M. (2010). *Formative assessment strategies for every classroom: An ASCD action tool* (2nd ed.). Alexandria, VA: ASCD.

Clinton, B. (2009). Inspect what you expect. Retrieved March 15, 2019, from http://www.greatleadershipbydan.com/2009/08/inspect-what-you-expect.html.

Hailikari, T., Katajavuori, N., & Lindblom-Ylanne, S. (2008). The relevance of prior knowledge in learning and instructional design. *American Journal of Pharmaceutical Education, 72*(5), 113.

Harlen, W. (2005). Teacher's summative practices and assessment for learning – tensions and Synergies. *Curriculum Journal, 16*(2), 207–23.

Harlen, W. & James, M. (1997). Assessment and learning: Differences and relationships between formative and summative assessment. *Assessment in Education: Principles, Policy & Practice, 4*(3), 365–79.

Harris, A., Jones, M., Cheah, K., Devadason, E., & Adams, D. (2017). Exploring principals' instructional leadership practices in Malaysia: Insights and implications. *Journal of Educational Administration, 55*(2), 207–21.

Herman, J., Osmundson, E., & Dietel, R. (2010). *Benchmark assessments for improved learning* (Issue brief). Retrieved March 13, 2019, from Assessment and Accountability Comprehensive Center website: https://files.eric.ed.gov/fulltext/ED524108.pdf (ERIC Document Reproduction Service).

Hicks, M. (2013). Interim assessments—What they are and how to use them to benefit student learning. Retrieved March 13, 2019, from https://www.nwea.org/blog/2013/interim-assessments-use-benefit-student-learning/.

Hockett, J. & Doubet, K. (2013). Turning on the lights: What pre-assessments can do. *Educational Leadership, 71*(4), 50–54.

Hoy, A., Davis, H., & Pape, S. (2006). Teacher knowledge and beliefs. In: P. A. Alexander & P. H. Winne (eds.). *Handbook of educational psychology* (pp. 715–38). New York, NY: Routledge.

Jacobs, H. H. (1996). *Mapping the big picture: Integrating curriculum and assessment k-12.* Alexandria, VA: ASCD.

King, K. & Zucker, S. (2005). *Curriculum narrowing.* Harcourt Assessments, Retrieved March 12, 2019, from images.pearsonclinical.com/images/PDF/assessmentReports/CurriculumNarrowing.pdf.

Leithwood, K., Day, C., Sammons, P., Hopkins, D., & Harris, A. (2006). *Successful school leadership: What it is and how it influences pupil learning.* London: DfES.

Lewis, C. (2009). What is the nature of knowledge development in lesson study? *Educational Action Research, 17*(1), 95–110.

Olson, L. (2005). Benchmark assessments offer regular checkups on student achievement. Retrieved March 15, 2019, from http://www.edweek.org/ew/articles/2005/11/30/13benchmark.h25.html.

Pendergrass, E. (2013). Differentiation: It starts with pre-assessment. *Educational Leadership, 71*(4).

Reeves, D. (2001). *101 questions & answers about standards, assessment, and accountability.* Englewood, CO: Advanced Learning Press.

Shen, J., Poppink, S., Cui, Y., & Fan, G. (2007). Lesson planning: A practice of professional responsibility and development. *Educational Horizons, 85*(4), 248–58.

Squires, D. (2012). Curriculum alignment research suggests that alignment can improve student achievement. *The Clearing House: A Journal of Educational Strategies, Issues, and Ideas, 85*(4), 129–35,

Tschannen-Moran, M. & Gareis, C. (2015). Faculty trust in the principal; an essential ingredient in high-performing schools. *Journal of Educational Administration, 53*(1), 66–92.

Tygret, J. A. (2018). The preparation and education of first-year teachers: A case study. *The Qualitative Report, 23*(3), 710–29. Retrieved from https://nsuworks.nov a.edu/tqr/vol23/iss3/15.

Webb, N. (1997). *Research monograph number 6: Criteria for alignment of expectations and assessments on mathematics and science education.* Washington, DC: CCSSO.

Webb, N. (2002). *Depth-of-knowledge levels for four content areas.* Retrieved March 15, 2019, from http://facstaff.wcer.wisc.edu/normw/All content areas DOK levels 32802.pdf.

Wiggins, G. & McTighe, J. (2011). *The understanding by design guide to creating high quality units.* Alexandria, VA: ASCD.

William, D. & Thompson, M. (2007). Integrating assessment with instruction: What will it take to make it work? In *The future of assessment: Shaping teaching and learning.* Mahwah, NJ: Lawrence Erlbaum Associates.

Zhukova, T. (2018). *Importance of English lesson planning. Pedagogy, Science, Research and Development East European Conference.* Barcelona, Spain.

Zook, C. (2017, December 14). Formative vs summative assessments: What's the difference? Retrieved March 27, 2019, from https://www.aeseducation.com/blog/f ormative-vs.-summative-assessments-what-do-they-mean.

Chapter 3

Alignment of Assessments

Good teaching is more of giving the right questions than a giving of right answers.

—*Josef Albers*

COGNITIVE ALIGNMENT OF ASSESSMENTS

Once the standards are unpacked and teachers understand what the desired outcomes are, the next step is to align the assessments. According to Wiggins and McTighe (2011) and Reynolds and Kearns (2016), the backward by design approach requires three steps:

1. Identify desired results—unwrapping the standards
2. Determine Assessment Evidence—assessment alignment
3. Plan Instruction—instructional alignment

This method has been followed in this book in regard to curriculum and instruction. First, one must establish the learner outcomes, and then one must determine that assessment evidence.

Too often, teachers rely on commercially produced materials for assessments, and unfortunately, they are not always aligned to the learning objective. Therefore, it is imperative to view the assessments prior to teaching and make adjustments, if necessary, or even start from scratch. Think of your assessments as a roadmap to teaching your unit. Building the assessments first will keep teachers on track during the unit and ensure that students are gaining the knowledge they need.

On Task versus On Target

Teachers need to know how to create aligned assessment items, and it is hard work. Once teachers understand the assessment demands of the standards, they can work to tweak existing items to make them aligned. Time savers are morale boosters. One must first determine if an assessment item is on *task* or on *target*. In order to do so, teachers must fully understand the cognitive level of the standard. Those items that are *on task* merely address the topic of the standard presented; whereas, those items that are *on target* assess the cognitive demand of the standard.

This process takes some thought and study of the standards that was addressed in the prior chapter. Take a look at a standard and a couple of assessment items for clarification. When looking at the questions, think about the cognitive demand of the standard in figure 3.1.

Both of these questions are considered to be *on task* because they both address point of view in the question stem. When looking back at the standard, however, neither question is *on target*, in that they do not compare and/or contrast points of view; and neither asks how a point of view determines the author's meaning. A better example of a question for this standard is explained in figure 3.2.

In this case, the correct answer is E, all of the above. In the first passage, the third-person point of view allows the reader to see through the eyes of Red and Texas Joe, revealing character traits of both characters and the line of plot development. In the second story, the reader can only see through the eyes of the narrator.

With a first-person point of view, the author can veer from truth and become more creative in perceptions of reality. This is one impact that point of view can have on a story. Students have to understand the impact of points of view and recognize them in the stories presented. Therefore, this question is on target for the learning standard.

4-RL.11.1: Compare and contrast first and third person points of view; determine how an author's choice of point of view influences the content and meaning.

1. What is point of view?
   a. The vantage point or position from which a story is told.
   b. When the narrator is in the story.
   c. When the narrator is not in the story.
   d. A story with no perspective.

2. In what point of view does a character in the story retell his or her experiences from a personal perspective?
   a. First Person
   b. Second Person
   c. Third Person Limited
   d. Third Person Omniscient

Figure 3.1   Sample Standard and Assessment Items.

1.Read the two passages below and answer the following question.

Lone Wolves and Other Frontier Tales by S. Goodson

Red looked across the prairie. He didn't see anything concerning. He wondered why Texas Joe had hollered like that. Texas Joe turned to him. The ghost that Texas Joe had just seen was gone. Texas Joe swatted at the air. Now he felt crazy. "You have to believe me, Red. It was just here," said Texas Joe. Red scowled at him in disbelief. "What was just here, Joe?" he asked. Red was angry with Texas Joe for disturbing his sleep for no apparent reason.

Sugar Fever: The Candy Wars by Douglass Wimperford

We stared at the Bubblegum Fortress from the mouth of the Cotton Candy Woods. The gumdrop soldiers were scurrying atop their sugar-coated ramparts. I wouldn't be surprised if someone had tipped them off. Chet Eagle approached me and said, "What now, Commander Candy?" I thought about it for a second. "Well, they get better prepared with each passing second, so let's attack now." Chet Eagle bowed and said, "As you wish, Commander Candy."

---

1. In the above two passages, the authors use different points of view. What is the impact of the authors' choices?
   a. In the first story, the reader understands both characters' feelings.
   b. In the second story, the reader can see the development of the story through one person's eyes.
   c. The first story is written from an objective point of view.
   d. The second story is subjective and can be more creative.
   e. All of the above

Figure 3.2   Sample Aligned Assessment Item.

Alignment with Webb's DOK

Writing standards-aligned assessment items can be hard work, as previously stated, but it is critical work. In developing assessment items, it is helpful to utilize Webb's DOK. Webb (1997) developed a system to evaluate the dichotomy of expectation and assessment. Ensuring that assessments are aligned to expectations, or learner outcomes as defined by standards, allows the teacher to properly assess student learning.

Webb's DOK explains the level at which students must understand the content in order to use or apply the information. In 2002, Webb published "Depth of Knowledge in the Four Content Areas," in which he described how the DOK can be used in the four core content areas, and also established the following levels:

DOK 1: Recall and reproduction of data or knowledge acquisition
DOK 2: Use academic concepts to analyze texts, address problems, and so on or knowledge application
DOK 3: Use academic concepts to explain decisions, conclusions, and outcomes or knowledge analysis

DOK 4: Use academic concepts outside of learning context to use information in new contexts or knowledge augmentation.

When looking back at curriculum maps, it is helpful to include the DOK associated with each standard. This will guide teachers in assessment development as well. See figure 3.3 for the curriculum map with DOK levels.

Professional Development Activity

A good professional development challenges teachers to examine their own practice and how it can be improved. Try this one. Ask teachers to bring a

EII-RL.5.1/EII-RI.5.1 Cite strong and thorough textual evidence to support analysis of what the text says explicitly as well as inferences drawn from the text; identify multiple supported interpretations.				Additional Resources
Need to Know	Skills	What It Means	Required Resources	
Evidence Inference	Cite Identify	Cite Evidence **DOK 2**	A Shakespeare play such as *The Taming of the Shrew, Much Ado About Nothing, The Merchant of Venice* or *The Tragedy of Julius Caesar*	Close reading with JC https://www.folger.edu/close-reading-the-conspiracy-in-act-2 Folger' Library www.folger.edu http://www.shakespeare-online.com https://www.tes.com/teaching-shakespeare/themes/
EII-RL.12.2 Analyze how an author's choices concerning how to structure a text, order events within the text, and manipulate time to create different effects.				
Events Within the Text Manipulation of Time & Text Structure	Analyze	determine significance of text structure and manipulation of time **DOK 3**	Same as above or *Twelve Angry Men* by Reginald Rose	https://www.prestwickhouse.com/blog/post/2017/12/how-to-teach-twelve-angry-men http://www.samandscout.com/drama-and-persuasion-mini-unit-with-twelve-angry-men/ https://edsitement.neh.gov/launchpad-activities-twelve-angry-men
Concepts: Central idea, claim, counterclaim, rebuttal, evidence, false statements, reasoning				
Required Instructional Elements: Writing, Research, Close Reading				

Figure 3.3   Curriculum Map with DOK.

copy of one of their preferred assessments to a professional development as well as a copy of the state standards they were using in developing the assessment. During the session, ask teachers to do the following:

1. Label each question with the standard/indicator the question is to assess.
2. Determine how many questions for each indicator are represented on the assessment.
3. Determine if each assessment item is on task or on target.
4. Create a matrix for the evaluation. See figure 3.4 for an example of a matrix for an assessment that covered only five standards/indicators.

This task seems relatively simple, but it is enlightening. It allows teachers to see how many questions are being assessed per standard/indicator as well as determine if the questions are *on task* or *on target*. This exercise takes some teachers by complete surprise. They may find that the majority of their questions are on task rather than on target, and some questions are not even represented in the standards at all. Also, teachers may find that the standards addressed in the assessment did not assess the standards intended to be assessed in the unit.

Furthermore, this exercise can demonstrate that the number of questions asked per standard is often insufficient to determine proficiency. This leads to the conversation about proficiency. Can you really determine if a student has mastered a standard with only one or two questions for that standard?

More about this topic will follow in the chapter on using data to inform instruction. However, the exercise is powerful in that teachers learn that assessments have to be cognitively aligned in order to ensure students are learning at the cognitive level the standards demand.

TYPES OF ASSESSMENTS

The question then arises if all assessments have to be *on target*. The answer is not necessarily. If teachers' assessments are mostly *on task,* then changing all of the assessment to be *on target* will shock students and negatively impact achievement results. In this case, the discussion about a sliding scale can ensue.

This means that if 75 percent of items are *on task*, then the teacher can start with 50 percent of items *on target* to begin. Gradual release to more items *on target* will give the teacher the opportunity to retrain the brains of her students to use more higher-order thinking skills. Jumping right into *on target* assessments will only frustrate students and the teacher.

Standard Matrix for On Target Assessment Items

_____ 1.1 _____1.2 _____1.3 _____2.4 _____2.5

Standards Matrix for On Task Assessment Items

_____ 1.1 _____1.2 _____1.3 _____2.4 _____2.5

Assessment Items Not Addressed in Standards/Indicators:

Figure 3.4   Assessment Standard Matrix.

Students do need the opportunity to practice the skills at the cognitive level of the standard prior to being tested on them. Students also need a multitude of opportunities to demonstrate their learning prior to a summative assessment. Let's look at the types of assessments that should guide instruction.

Pre-assessment

Pre-assessments are those assessments given prior to teaching a unit. The purpose of these assessments is to see what students know and do not know. This will help guide the differentiation process in addition to sparking some interest in the subject to be taught (Hocket & Doubet, 2014; Pendergrass,

2013). If students, through a few questions, can inform the teacher that they already have knowledge of a subject or possess a skill, the teacher may then decide to spend less time on that subject and more on another about which the students were less informed; teachers may also decide to create learning groups based on prior knowledge.

This pre-assessment can also inform the teacher about instructional supplies and materials needed for the unit. Of course, the results of this assessment are for information purposes only, not to be used as a graded assignment. Often, the pre-assessment step in planning instruction is skipped due to the time crunch teachers feel to teach all of their standards; however, these same teachers fail to realize they could be saving instructional time by spending less time on matter or skipping areas students already are proficient.

Pre-assessments help create a more productive classroom by saving time and resources, help to focus instruction on the areas needed, and help set the stage for students on the learning to come (Hailikari, Katajavuori, & LIndblom-Ylanne, 2008; Hockett & Doubet, 2013). These assessments do not have to be cognitively aligned to the standards, as they are intended to inform the teacher about any background knowledge the students may possess on the topic.

Formative Assessments

Formative assessments should be used frequently and should include a wide variety of types. These assessments are intended to inform the teacher about the progress of student learning toward a learning goal at various times in the learning process, prior to a unit assessment or test. These assessments need to be cognitively aligned to the standards, as these assessments should mirror what is expected on the summative assessments. According to Brookhart (2010) and Dixson and Worrell (2016), students need and deserve opportunities to learn before they are graded. That is the purpose of regular formative assessments.

Teachers should plan these formative assessments in advance so as not to skip this important step in the learning process due to time constraints. Additionally, teachers should add formative assessments if they see that students are not grasping an idea wholly in order to determine where the weakness in understanding lies. In essence, formative assessments should occur during and between learning. William and Thompson (2007) state that formative assessments consist of five key strategies:

1. Clarifying and sharing learning intentions and criteria for success
2. Engineering effective classroom discussions and other learning tasks that elicit evidence of student understanding
3. Providing feedback that moves learners forward
4. Activating students as instructional resources for one another
5. Activating students as the owners of their own learning

In essence, formative assessments inform the students as to their progress toward the learning goal as well as inform the teacher of instructional synchronous effectiveness. Additionally, some formative assessment strategies, such as group work, also allow the students to serve as resources to one another on the learning continuum, which can operate as a motivating factor for students to learn and to own their own learning (Black & William, 2009).

Formative assessments take many shapes and styles and a plethora of resources exist to help develop formative assessments in the classroom. See table 3.1 for a chart of some free, available resources on formative assessments. Administrators should set instructional expectations for teachers as to how many formative assessments must be planned and executed prior to a summative assessment. Now, these formative assessment expectations have to be set at a minimum level because teachers need to feel free to give more than the minimum prescribed.

This type of instructional expectation school policy should be made with a school's Leadership Team in order to create ownership of the expectations. One class period could result in a multitude of formative assessments, easily. Each one given should inform the instruction that comes next. As a result, a teacher should know what students comprehend prior to giving a summative assessment.

Mid-term Assessments or Benchmarks

Benchmark assessments should serve four functions for teachers, students, and administrators: (1) communicate learning expectations, (2) plan curriculum and instruction, (3) monitor/evaluate program effectiveness, and (4) predict future performance of students (Black & William, 1998; Herman, Osmundson, & Dietel, 2010). Every assessment communicates learning expectations to students and should be used to plan curriculum and instruction, but not all assessments will predict future performance and afford the opportunity to evaluate program effectiveness.

There are two types of benchmarks: those that measure the same set of knowledge at different points in the year to predict future performance on state tests and those that measure the specific standards and skills taught during a specified period of time.

The hazard with the first type of benchmark assessment is that teachers may just teach to that specific set of knowledge standards and never go in-depth with any other standards. With the latter type of benchmark, teachers are analyzing results to determine their effectiveness within a specified time period. This information allows for teachers to remediate needed instruction of all standards within the curriculum map in a timely fashion, whereas the first type of benchmark may assess standards not taught within the timeframe of the benchmark administration (Olson, 2005; Hicks, 2013).

Table 3.1 Resources on Formative Assessments

Source	Title	Site
NCTE	Formative Assessments That *Truly* Inform Instruction	http://www.ncte.org/library/NCTEFiles/Resources/Positions/formative-assessment_single.pdf
Common Sense Education	Make Formative Assessment More Student Centered	https://www.commonsense.org/education/teaching-strategies/student-centered-formative-assessment
Sixty Formative Assessment Strategies	Improving Student Learning in the CTE Classrooms Through Formative Assessments	https://1.cdn.edl.io/SMr2qJk2AGiVvUuTLMGhN02CY9DN774AogEBmti2GcbMeEmu.pdf
NWEA	Twenty-seven Easy Formative Assessment Strategies for Gathering Evidence of Student Learning	https://www.nwea.org/blog/2019/27-easy-formative-assessment-strategies-for-gathering-evidence-of-student-learning/
Edutopia	Fifty-six Examples of Formative Assessments	https://www.edutopia.org/groups/assessment/250941
Northern Arizona University	Formative Assessment Strategies, Definitions, and Examples	https://nau.edu/uploadedFiles/Academic/CAL/History/History-Social_Studies_Education/Formative%20Assessment%20Strategies%20Definitions%20Examples.pdf
Boston Public Schools	Formative (Informal) Assessment Strategies	https://www.bostonpublicschools.org/cms/lib07/MA01906464/Centricity/Domain/44/Formative_Informal.pdf
DreamBox Learning	Formative Assessment Toolkit	https://www.eschoolnews.com/files/2018/03/tk-16-06-dreambox_formative_assessment.pdf
Council of Chief State School Officers	Formative Assessments For Students With Disabilities	https://ccsso.org/sites/default/files/2017-12/Formative_Assessment_for_Students_with_Disabilities.pdf
NWEA	Seventy-five Digital Tools and Apps Teachers Can Use to Support Formative Assessment In The Classroom	https://www.nwea.org/blog/2019/75-digital-tools-apps-teachers-use-to-support-classroom-formative-assessment/
The TechEdvocate	Eleven EdTech Tools That Make Formative Assessment A Breeze	https://www.thetechedvocate.org/11-edtech-tools-make-formative-assessment-breeze/
Maryland Online	Formative Assessment Tools	https://www.qualitymatters.org/qa-resources/resource-center/articles-resources/formative-assessment-tools

(Continued)

Table 3.1 **Resources on Formative Assessments** (*Continued*)

Source	Title	Site
Educational Technology and Mobile Learning	Here Are Some Of The Best Formative Assessment Tools for Teachers	https://www.educatorstechnology.com/2018/01/here-are-some-of-best-formative.html
Teaching Channel	Formative Assessment Resources: Try Them Today, Tomorrow, Or Sometime Soon	https://www.teachingchannel.org/blog/2015/03/04/formative-assessment-resources
Prodigy	Twenty Formative Assessment Examples	https://www.prodigygame.com/blog/formative-assessment-examples/
School Leaders Now	Nine Informal Assessments That Help Administrators Pinpoint What Learners Need	https://schoolleadersnow.weareteachers.com/useful-formative-assessment/

The latter type of benchmark affords a paradigm shift in teacher ownership and student ownership in learning. Teachers taught the material, but were they effective for the specific students at that specific time? It is not unusual for a fantastic teacher to plan and execute a lesson to perfection and have it fail miserably. This is normal behavior. For each student comes to class with different skills and talents. However, the work of remediation begins here.

Teachers need to understand that failure is allowed as long as teachers then back up and punt and reteach. Students need to understand that the latter type of benchmark only assesses what has been taught to that point, and they are responsible for having learned that material. Students themselves may need to back up and punt as well. With either type of benchmark, teachers nor students should be surprised with state exam results. When more than one teacher is giving the same benchmark, say English 2, teachers can analyze the data to inform best practices as well as identify standards with which they are having difficulty.

Administrators can use the data as well by observing patterns of behavior. If one standard is troublesome for all teachers in that subject area, then maybe there is a curricular issue or an assessment alignment issue. Do teachers need additional professional development on these standards? Do teachers need additional materials and resources? These types of questions can easily be answered with benchmark data.

In giving benchmark assessments that assessed the standards taught during a specified period of time, an administrator is able to see what standards the staff is strong in teaching and what standards need to be revisited. These patterns across teachers highlight spending needs, professional development needs, as well as deserved accolades.

Teachers are able to see remediation needs as well. Data meetings should be held after each benchmark assessment to look at departmental data. Each teacher can see each other's data, and fruitful conversations follow about how teachers teach certain standards. Brainstorming sessions ensue on how to correct standards that are weak.

Additionally, administrators and teachers can see patterns across subject levels. For example, during a math data meeting, a principal may notice that Algebra 1, Algebra 2, and Pre-Calculus all have the same weakness—factoring. As a result, the entire department may focus on factoring in all three courses, and teachers can assess understanding multiple times to ensure proficiency.

Brainstorming sessions can follow on how to teach factoring in the multiple courses as well. This focus will help not only the students that teachers are serving at that point but also future students. These data meetings after benchmark assessments provide some of the best professional development and teacher collaboration opportunities.

Administrators need to decide how often benchmark, or interim, assessments should be given in the school, no matter the type of benchmark. If an administrator decides to give a benchmark that covers specific standards on multiple occasions for the purposes of predicting outcomes on state assessments, then that data should be reviewed each time to see if students are growing in their understanding and application of those subject standards.

Summative Assessments

Formative assessments are used to evaluate learning during the teaching process, and results are used to inform instruction through a unit, or for learning. However, summative assessments are used to evaluate the learning that occurred at the end of a unit or course (Zook, 2017; Harlen & James, 2006; Broadfoot & Black, 2004). Summative assessments include tests, projects, papers, and the like. However, the argument can be made that though summative assessments are needed, teachers shouldn't turn the page and never look back.

Are students not responsible to learn what they did not to that point? Surely, teachers continue to remediate because some students just take longer to learn than others (Harlen, 2005). As such, the only real summative assessment should be the final exam. All other assessments, including unit assessments, should be treated as formative assessments, despite where in the instructional process they occur.

As previously addressed, teachers may need to back up and punt when using formative assessment data that tells the teacher students did not understand the material. If a teacher consistently uses formative assessment data to inform daily instruction, then the summative assessment data throughout the course provides an opportunity for students to back up and punt as well.

Of course, if a teacher notices that the majority of students did not understand a standard/indicator, the teacher should back up and punt, again. Opportunity exists for the teacher to confer with other teachers to determine best practices. With the advent of "No Zero" and redo policies in schools, again, the only real summative assessment is the final exam in a course.

SYSTEMS PERSPECTIVE

The same IT discussed in chapter 2 should be utilized when examining assessments. Lesson plans were discussed in the last chapter and the importance of administrators reviewing lesson plans prior to the instructional period they cover. Also discussed was the use of Wiggin's and McTighe's (2011) backward by design approach to planning.

So, if teachers are beginning with the end in mind (Reeves, 2001), it would stand to reason that assessments are attached to lesson plans prior to the designated instructional period beginning. This does require that teachers truly plan well in advance; however, once the planning is done, the instruction is more efficient.

In the weekly meetings with your IT, lesson plans and assessments should be discussed. Remember, the team must decide on the frequency of assessments required in your building. With this school policy, the system approach ensures that the policy is followed and students are given ample opportunities to practice prior to summative assessments. The system for Alignment of Assessments will look like what is illustrated in figure 3.5.

PROGRESS MONITORING

The benefits of administrators viewing the assessments with the lesson plans are plentiful. Though viewing assessments with lesson plans takes more time, the effort is worth it. Plus, teachers took the time to develop the assessments up front; therefore, administrators must value their time and effort as well. Benefits include the following:

a. Highlights if formative assessments are cognitively aligned to standards/indicators.
b. Determines the number and type of formative assessments if sufficient opportunities to learn were presented in lesson.
c. Determines if instructional strategies are cognitively aligned to standards/indicators.
d. Determines if summative assessments are aligned to standards/indicators.
e. Determine when assessments will be given.

Common errors in the learning process occur with insufficient opportunities with formative assessments, in particular with formative assessments not aligned to the cognitive level of the standards. For example, the math teacher who consistently gives students linear math problems to solve but assesses

Figure 3.5   System for Alignment of Assessments.

student understanding on a summative assessment in the context of word problems reflecting real-world experiences is setting the students up to fail.

Meaning, homework that is consistently checked for completion does not serve a diagnostic purpose for students or teachers. If homework is intended to be used as a formative assessment, then it must be checked for accuracy. A teacher who consistently utilizes a "thumbs up, thumbs down" formative assessment will never know what her students truly know and don't know. Students inherently will not want to be embarrassed and admit they don't know the material when their classmates do.

Also, students sometimes "go along to get along" and move on. Therefore, it is imperative that teachers use a myriad of formative assessments for real diagnostic purposes, and those assessments must be aligned to what the expectations will be on the summative assessment. If they are not, students are not trained on what to expect. This is not teaching to the test, but rather preparing students to meet the expectations.

Lastly, administrators typically do not like to observe during a test because they are not seeing the teacher teach; however, that time can be viewed differently. Observing during an assessment gives an administrator a bird's-eye view of student behavior during the test. If students are working diligently, then it is apparent that the students are confident with the material. If students are struggling and the frustration is visible, then maybe there was a problem during the instruction and the use of the formative assessment data.

Sometimes, teachers will report that students did well throughout the unit and bombed the final assessment. How can this be? If the assessments are aligned and students have been given ample opportunity to practice, this should not happen too often. The assessment itself is oftentimes the problem. Viewing them in advance can prevent some of this frustration for both the teacher and the students.

SUMMARY

Curriculum and assessment are critical components of the instructional system. Curriculum maps and unit organizers guide teachers on what to teach, not how to teach; so, teachers still have flexibility in their classrooms. Assessments serve to inform students as to what is important for them to learn. An instructional system must direct these two components to ensure fidelity of instruction.

Curriculum guides and unit organizers should contain the unwrapped standards, the concepts students need to know, the skills they need to be able to do, the cognitive demand of the standards, the DOK demands of the teaching targets, required resources, and supplemental resources. Assessments should include pre-assessments, a multitude of formative assessments, benchmark assessments, and summative assessments.

The formative and summative assessments must be cognitively aligned so that students have many opportunities to reach the desired outcomes prior to a summative assessment. Benchmark assessments, also cognitively aligned, serve to inform the teacher and administrator on program effectiveness to that point.

All assessments provide useful data to inform instruction. An administrator must progress monitor this system through lesson plan review, observation, and data meetings.

A PIECE AT A TIME

Consider the following after reading this chapter:

- Do your teachers turn in assessments with their lesson plans?
- Are assessments cognitively aligned to the standards (on target vs. on task)?
- Do teachers give enough (aligned) formative assessments? How do you know?
- How do your teachers use unit assessments? Are they formative or summative?
- What are the instructional expectations in your school? How do you monitor and support teachers with the expectations?

REFERENCES

Black, P. & William, D. (1998). Assessment and classroom learning. *Educational Assessment: Principles, Policy & Practice, 5*(1), 7–74.

Black, P. & William, D. (2009). Developing the theory of formative assessment. *Educational Assessment, Evaluation and Accountability, 1*(1), 5–31.

Blasé, J. (2000). Effective instructional leadership: Teachers' perspectives on how principals promote teaching and learning in schools. *Journal of Educational Administration, 38*(2), 130–41.

Broadfoot, P. & Black, P. (2004). Redefining assessment? The first ten years of assessment in education. *Assessment in Education: Principles, Policy & Practice, 11*(1), 7–26.

Dixson, D. & Worrell, F. (2016). Formative and summative assessments in the classroom. *Theory Into Practice, 55*(2), 153–59.

Hailikari, T., Katajavuori, N., & Lindblom-Ylanne, S. (2008). The relevance of prior knowledge in learning and instructional design. *American Journal of Pharmaceutical Education, 72*(5), 113.

Harlen, W. (2005). Teacher's summative practices and assessment for learning—tensions and synergies. *Curriculum Journal, 16*(2), 207–23.

Harlen, W. & James, M. (1997). Assessment and learning: Differences and relationships between formative and summative assessment. *Assessment in Education: Principles, Policy & Practice, 4*(3), 365–79.

Herman, J., Osmundson, E., & Dietel, R. (2010). *Benchmark assessments for improved learning* (Issue brief). Retrieved March 13, 2019, from Assessment and Accountability Comprehensive Center website: https://files.eric.ed.gov/fulltext/ ED524108.pdf (ERIC Document Reproduction Service).

Hicks, M. (2013). Interim assessments—What they are and how to use them to benefit student learning. Retrieved March 13, 2019, from https://www.nwea.org/blog/2013 /interim-assessments-use-benefit-student-learning/.

Hockett, J. & Doubet, K. (2013). Effective pre-assessments can illuminate where students are now so that teachers can lead them to mastery. *Educational Leadership, 71*(4), 50–54.

Hocket, J. & Doubet, K. (2014). Turning on the lights: What pre-assessments can do. *Educational Leadership, 71*(4), 50–54.

Olson, L. (2005). Benchmark assessments offer regular checkups on student achievement. Retrieved March 15, 2019, from http://www.edweek.org/ew/articles/2005/1 1/30/13benchmark.h25.html.

Pendergrass, E. (2013). Differentiation: It starts with pre-assessment. *Educational Leadership, 71*(4).

Reeves, D. (2001). *101 questions & answers about standards, assessment, and accountability.* Englewood, CO: Advanced Learning Press.

Reynolds, H. & Kearns, K. (2016). A planning tool for incorporating backward design, active learning, and authentic assessment in the college classroom. *College Teaching, 65*(1), 17–27.

Webb, N. (1997). *Research monograph number 6: Criteria for alignment of expectations and assessments on mathematics and science education.* Washington, DC: CCSSO.

Webb, N. (2002). *Depth-of-knowledge levels for four content areas.* Retrieved March 15, 2019, from http://facstaff.wcer.wisc.edu/normw/All content areas DOK levels 32802.pdf.

Wiggins, G. & McTighe, J. (2011). *The understanding by design guide to creating high quality units.* Alexandria, VA: ASCD.

William, D. & Thompson, M. (2007). Integrating assessment with instruction: What will it take to make it work? In *The future of assessment: Shaping teaching and learning.* Mahwah, NJ: Lawrence Erlbaum Associates.

Zook, C. (2017, December 14). Formative vs. summative assessments: What's the difference? Retrieved March 27, 2019, from https://www.aeseducation.com/blog/f ormative-vs.-summative-assessments-what-do-they-mean.

Chapter 4

Instructional Alignment

If you go to work on your goals, your goals will go to work on you.
If you go to work on your plan, your plan will go to work on you.
Whatever good things we build end up building us.

—*Jim Rohn*

This book has addressed the fact that understanding what the standards are asking of students and then creating the assessments first are critical steps in the teaching process. However, the most overlooked step in the instructional planning process is the alignment of instructional strategies. Why do you think that is?

Crafting instructional strategies that match the cognitive level of the standards often removes the teacher from the didactic mode of teaching, in which the teacher is the disseminator of knowledge and the students are more passive learners. This mode of instruction is most common because it is the most comfortable, where the teacher's knowledge is not questioned. In essence, teachers have control.

However, standards today have increased rigor with expectations of critical thought and problem solving; consequently, students then must be engaged learners who think independently and question processes. To create this level of engagement, teachers have to release responsibility to the students and let the students take the lead.

MAPPING

In order to ensure that instructional strategies are aligned, teachers must map the strategies that will result in the cognitive demand required. Often, the skills needed have to be scaffolded in the learning process, meaning students may need some background knowledge in order to assimilate the information required (Fisher & Frey, 2010). This is why it is so important to unwrap the standards first in the instructional planning process. The same process that is used to "begin with the end in mind" can be used when developing strategies (Reeves, 2001).

Teachers can see what is expected of the students in the standard; however, teachers need to backward map the strategies that will build students to the cognitive demand of the standard. For example, look at the eighth-grade science standard in the following.

Standard 8.E.4: The student will demonstrate an understanding of the universe and the predictable patterns caused by Earth's movement in the solar system.

What supporting standards are necessary for students to be able to demonstrate this understanding? What concepts must they know in order to discuss predictable patterns? The teacher must map the standards and supporting standards out, including key terms and the DOK levels first (like discussed in unit planning). See table 4.1 for a sample planning map.

It is important to note that the key terms/vocabulary should not be taught in isolation, as the standards do not ask students to define the concepts, but

Table 4.1   Sample Planning Map

Standard 8.E.4: The student will demonstrate an understanding of the universe and the predictable patterns caused by Earth's movement in the solar system.

Supporting Standards	DOK Level	Key Terms
8.E.4B.1 Obtain and communicate information to model and compare the characteristics and movements of objects in the solar system (including planets, moons, asteroids, comets, and meteors).	DOK 2 Understand Apply DOK 4 Model Compare	solar system, planets, moons, asteroids, comets, meteors, meteorite
8.E.4B.2 Construct explanations for how gravity affects the motion of objects in the solar system and tides on Earth.	DOK 2 Understand Construct	gravity, neap tides, tilt, axis, day, year, elliptical, orbit,
8.E.4B.4 Develop and use models to explain how motions within the Sun-Earth-Moon system cause Earth phenomena (including day and year, moon phases, solar and lunar eclipses, and tides).	DOK 2 Understand Model	lunar movement, phases of the moon, eclipses, solar, lunar, tide
8.E.4B.6 Analyze and interpret data from the surface features of the Sun (including photosphere, corona, sunspots, prominences, and solar flares) to predict how these features may affect Earth.	DOK 4 Analyze Interpret	photosphere, corona, sunspot, prominence, solar flares

to use the concepts. Therefore, teachers need to understand how to teach academic vocabulary without consuming instructional time on strategies that do not net the intended goals. When teachers put notes on the board (digital or otherwise) and have students copy them or have students write the definitions from the textbook in a notebook, students are not engaged in the learning at all and likely do not retain the information.

Often, teachers simply provide one avenue of reinforcement for students to memorize terms. Bretzing and Kulhary (1979) found that students who took notes verbatim comprehended less than those who engaged in higher-order thinking while taking notes. So, how can teachers up the ante with student learning?

One vocabulary method that creates the latter scenario might include having the student draw a picture or representation of the concept/term and put the definition in their own words which creates a deeper understanding of the concept (Marzano, 2009). Teachers have to be careful in using this strategy in that the entire assignment is not based on drawing illustrations but infusing that vocabulary development in the larger context of the material. Teachers who commonly use flip books, that include illustrations for terms, do not realize the low-level DOK of the planned activity.

Another tried and true method is for students to use interactive notebooks, which has proven to help students make connections to material and what the

Table 4.2   Sample Interactive Notebook Format

Left Side of Notebook	Right Side of Notebook
Notes in Student's Own Words (drawings/illustrations)	Notes from Teacher
Explain new vocabulary terms in own Words /drawings/illustrations	Underline new vocabulary terms used in notes
Questions student still has? What might someone else not understand?	Student writes summary

Table 4.3   **Functions and Associated Questions**

DOK Level	Function	Questions
1	Remember, State, Recall, Define	What?
2	Compare, Infer, Describe, Explain	How? Why?
3	Hypothesize, Investigate Support conclusions with details	What conclusions?
4	Analyze, Prove, Connect	New comparison? New uses?

material means to them (Caine, 2005; Wrobleski, 1985). In using interactive notebooks in schools, teachers found that the layout determined if the students achieved the intended goals. Students engage with the subject matter in interactive notebooks, and this practice informs the teacher on what students still need to understand, serving as a sound formative assessment for teachers.

Many resources exist to help teachers learn how to teach academic vocabulary, such as Janet Allen's *Tools for Teaching Academic Vocabulary* (2014). See table 4.2 for sample interactive notebook format. Now, remember, DOK levels will determine the learner outcomes or what the students are required to do with the information, and these levels should be represented in the assessments.

From this point, teachers can start to plan instructional strategies. The first step is to determine the function of the DOK levels and the types of question that would accompany the levels. For example, a DOK Level 1 assessment will focus on remembering, whereas a DOK Level 2 assessment will focus on applying or comparing. See table 4.3 for examples of functions and associated questions.

Next, teachers can start to plan strategies that meet the demands of the function and answer the questions associated with the standards. Looking back at the aforementioned science standard, teachers may employ strategies like the ones found in table 4.3.

DOK 2—Have students work in groups to investigate the lunar cycle and local tide maps. Then, students incorporate the knowledge of the tilt of the earth's axis and rotation to explain how all concepts affect one another. Students present to class their findings in poster form.

1. DOK 2—Have students create Venn diagrams based on movies that illustrate scientific principals as compared to the actual phenomena. Movies might include the following:
   a. *The Perfect Storm*
   b. *Solar Flare*
   c. *The Knowing*
   d. *The Day After Tomorrow*
   e. *Deep Impact*
   f. *Armageddon*

DOK 4—Have students investigate the concepts of photosphere, corona, sunspot, prominence, and solar flares. Students are assigned one concept to predict the outcome of the concept on their hometown to include statistics and scientific findings on impact and effects, in the form of one of the following (students chose):

a. Newspaper article
b. News broadcast with script performed in class
c. Presidential briefing
d. Essay
e. Short Story
f. Song

To use any of these strategies, teachers would have to develop the rubrics associated with each assignment. Of course, teachers will have to build students' abilities to meet these cognitive demands. In order to have students investigate the concepts, like in the second assignment, students will need to know how to research, how to read graphs and charts, and what questions need answering. These skills will transfer to other subjects as well.

Students, in turn, are actively engaged in the learning process, and the teacher can become the facilitator of knowledge, assisting students in the right direction and answering questions when needed. Additionally, teachers should model the expectations for each type of assignment so that students are clear about the expectations.

DIFFERENTIATED STRATEGIES

Everyone knows that kids learn differently and at different paces. One of the hardest things for teachers is understanding how to manage differentiation of instruction despite the fact that teachers often know what they need to do to meet the needs of learners. What teachers do not always understand is that they differentiate more than they think. Additionally, using assessment data effectively opens the door to better differentiation. There are many ways to differentiate instruction.

Create Lessons Based on Students' Learning Styles

Students have different strengths and weaknesses, and learning styles vary depending on their strengths. Matching learning styles with instructional strategies is another way to ensure students are more engaged in the learning because a learning style is simply a preference in how a student learns, not that a student cannot learn with other styles (Brown, 2000; Donggun & Carr, 2017). However, mismatched teaching styles and learning styles can decrease student motivation to learn over time (Letele, Alexander, & Swanepoel, 2013; Gilakjani, 2012). So, teachers need to inform students about the different styles and ask them as well as observe their preferences.

In the past, learning styles were categorized into four categories:

1. Visual—preference for pictures and images to explain concepts; need to see the connections to learn the material well
2. Auditory—preference for sound and music; need to hear it or say it to learn the material well
3. Tactile—preference is to write it down; need to write notes or write down what they have learned
4. Kinesthetic—preference is to learn through motion; need hands-on experiences to learn the material well (Kolb, 1984).

Teachers employ several of these methods often with graphic organizers, lecture, video, notes, models, and so on. However, the one area that is most often preferred, kinesthetic, is the learning style that is planned for the least (Tomlinson & McTighe, 2006).

Maybe this phenomenon exists because teachers do not know how to plan more hands-on activities, or maybe they feel loss of control over the classroom. Surely, evidence exists out there to support both assertions. However, research does show that students in poverty and at-risk students predominately prefer a kinesthetic approach to learning (Honigsfeld & Dunn, 2009). Ramifications of that research were highlighted by Kuykendall (2004):

> Students who find their culture and learning styles reflected in both the substance and organization of the instructional program are more likely to be motivated, less likely to be disruptive and more likely to benefit from their learning experience. (p. 71)

More recently, research has shifted gears on learning styles and now includes seven different learning styles, whereas three additional styles were added to the Kolb's four:

5. Logical—preference for logic and reasoning
6. Social—preference to work in groups or with others
7. Solitary—preference to work alone (Brualdi, 1998)

Implications of Gardner's work for teachers are critical to examine. How many times do teachers assign group work that only frustrates students? The opposite could be asked as well. In planning, teachers need to plan for each type of learning preference to maximize student engagement, and often this results in choice for students.

The addition of student choice in assignments gives students ownership of their learning and enhances critical thinking and allows for differentiation (Hanewicz, Platt, & Arendt, 2017). Additionally, students are more invested in their success when they get to choose the work to be done. Adults are no different, but yet students are expected to behave differently for some reason.

Group Students by Shared Interests or Abilities

Teachers find themselves assigning students to work in groups all the time. Often, students are left to self-select their groups, and this usually occurs based on friendships or the feeling that one student will carry the weight for the group. However, imagine grouping students based on a preferred topic or interest. For example, students who are given the choice of assignments based on the science standards listed earlier in this chapter may be grouped based on the love of action movies, artistic ability, creative writing, musical ability, or even a flare for the dramatic.

Additionally, those students who prefer to work in isolation may want to do the research and write an essay. In providing choice, students are able to rely on their strengths and interests to learn the material and demonstrate mastery of concepts.

Grouping students by ability can result in some high-level work; however, some caution needs to be advised. The rubric for the assignment or instructional expectations needs to be clearly defined and understood by the students and teacher prior to the beginning of the assignment. Students who have a higher ability level will surpass those expectations with little prodding, but the teacher must ensure that all groups can be successful.

In organizing these groups, the teacher can spend more time working with the lower-ability groups to guide the students through the process. By doing so, the teacher is working to elevate the levels of all groups in the classroom. This is truly a learner-centered approach and serves to provide real differentiation in the classroom.

Assess Students Through Formative Assessments

The types of formative assessments were addressed in the previous chapter, but more focus on the pre-assessment is warranted. A good pre-assessment is designed to inform the teacher and students. The assessment tells the students what will be addressed during the unit and apprises the teacher of any existing knowledge students have on the subject. Teachers are faced with a broad array of abilities and educational needs; as such, teachers can use this information to create learning groups, design curriculum and pacing, and allocate resources and materials effectively to positively impact student achievement (Goddard & Goddard, 2019; Moon, 2005).

As stated earlier, pre-assessments can serve to save teacher instructional time in the curricular unit. Creating groups based on prior knowledge differentiates instruction from the beginning of a unit (Levy, 2008), and this is found to be a powerful practice. How can teachers possibly plan to meet the needs of all students in advance of learning without a pre-assessment? Simply put, most teachers plan to meet the needs after students have failed.

Formative assessments that are given continuously throughout a unit allows the teacher to adjust instruction, back up and remediate as well as accelerate students based on their level of understanding. Of course, these formative assessments need to be administered frequently and should vary in type as long as they are cognitively aligned. Daily formative assessments provide the best data to inform instruction. Teachers just have to plan ahead and be prepared for the needed remediation and enrichment exercises. What better way to differentiate?

Remediating student learning using formative assessments dictates the ebb and flow of a classroom. Student groups may change frequently, based on the acquired understanding of the material. The teacher needs to be able to manage changing groups, just as the teacher needs to be prepared with materials to address the different needs of the students. Flexibility is a must, and this flexibility can only be executed smoothly with lots of advance planning.

SYSTEMS PERSPECTIVE

How do administrators develop a system to ensure that instructional strategies are aligned and are differentiated to meet the needs of students? Again, go back to lesson plan review. Using the same IT discussed in the previous chapters, discussing strategies becomes part of lesson plan review. These conversations need to become part of the school culture—how we operate.

So far, the instructional system includes curriculum mapping, alignment of assessments, and alignment of instructional strategies—all of which are part of the lesson plan review with the IT. Administrators must build time to have these hearty conversations in order to stress importance and value. To save some time during meetings, those on the team who have questions about strategies or assessments should speak to the teacher for clarification prior to the weekly meeting.

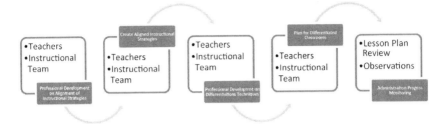

Figure 4.1   System for Aligned Instructional Strategies.

Sometimes, understanding comes through conversation, and these conversations help teachers to solidify the plans as well as inform administrators. Of course, the tone of the meeting with teachers is very important. A member of the IT should approach such a teacher meeting in a manner similar to the following:

> Miss Roberts, I really enjoyed reading your lesson plan this week. I am interested in how you are teaching these concepts. Can you walk me through your process? I think I would like to observe during this time!

In this approach, teachers can be excited about their teaching rather than defensive about their craft and expertise. A system for instructional alignment can look like figure 4.1.

PROGRESS MONITORING

As discussed, progress monitoring occurs with lesson plan review, but it also occurs with observation. Observations can be powerful tools if used properly. Further discussion about the different types of observations occurs later in the book, but for the purposes of this chapter, the focus is based on the observations of strategies.

In the example given earlier with the teacher, that IT member should observe during that time presented in the lesson plan. Lesson plan reviews highlight not only what the teachers will be teaching but also what the students will be doing as well. Patterns of behavior will emerge during your reviews and should be observed.

For example, Miss Roberts, a new teacher, often relies on the didactic teaching method. That pattern will emerge when reviewing her lesson plans and during observations. You may observe students taking notes from the board or during lecture, and feel like the teacher utilizes this strategy all too often. Walk in most American high schools and you will find this practice readily.

However, you realize that students' learning styles are not being addressed as well as the infrequent use of aligned formative assessments. From the observations, you can have a rich discussion on strategies you have observed and when they may be appropriate. You can continue the conversation with a brainstorming session on other strategies the teacher could utilize, providing support for the teacher.

On the other hand, you may find Miss Roberts's lesson plan appears very engaging for students, and you just have to see it for yourself. Observations based on these reviews often highlight best practices in the building that can and should be shared with other teachers. Tapping teachers to present professional development on best practices you observed is a huge morale booster and some of the best professional development money can buy.

The point is that lesson plan review and observations should tie together; they should not be haphazard and inconsistent. Combining the two in your progress monitoring system allows administrators to see patterns in the building and to identify areas of needed professional development for teachers. To do less just does not make sense and ensures that the two practices are disjointed and less meaningful.

Of course, members of the IT will observe teachers outside of their departments, but the IT members will become the curriculum resource for their departments. Teachers need to see IT members as resources, not a vehicle to micromanage teachers and catch them doing something wrong. If administrators are seen as an instructional resource, teachers' self-efficacy improves (Sehgal, Nambudiri, & Mishra, 2017).

SUMMARY

Teachers need to map instructional strategies just as they map curriculum. Mapping backward from the desired student outcomes, understanding the function of the standards and the questions associated with them, allows teachers to plan instructional strategies that can be scaffolded to best meet the needs of students. Differentiation of instruction is essential and occurs more than teachers think. There are several ways to differentiate: by learning preference, by groups based on interest or ability, and by using formative assessment data.

A combination of all three practices has the most powerful impact. Administrators need to include instructional strategies in the school's lesson plan policy so that alignment to the cognitive level of the standards is evident. Also, the inclusion of strategies to be used in lesson plans assists with instructional conversations based on review and observations. Alignment among all three components helps to ensure alignment in the classroom.

A PIECE AT A TIME

1. What elements are required in your lesson plans?
2. What patterns do you think you will see in your building?
3. Are teachers differentiating instruction effectively?
4. Is formative assessment data used to inform instruction?
5. How will you engage in those conversations so that teachers view them as developmental rather than critical?
6. What is the current role of your administration? Instructional Support or Managers of Instruction?

REFERENCES

Allen, J. (2014). *Tools for teaching academic vocabulary.* Portsmouth, NH: Stenhouse Publishers.

Bokyung, L. & Haedong, K. (2014). What can we learn from our learners' learning styles? *English Language Teaching, 7*(9), 118–31.

Bretzing, B. H. & Kulhary, R. W. (1979). Note-taking and depth of processing. *Contemporary Educational Psychology, 4*(2), 145–53.

Brown, H. D. (2000). *Principles of language learning and teaching* (4th ed.). New York, NY: Longman.

Brualdi, A. (1998). Garder's theory. *Teacher Librarian, 26*(2), 26–28.

Caine, R. M, Caine, G., McClintic, C., & Klimek, K. (2005). *12 Brain/mind learning principles in action: The field book for making connections, teaching and the human brain.* California: Corwin Press.

Donggun, A. & Carr, M. (2017). Learning styles theory fails to explain learning and achievement: Recommendations for alternative approaches. *Personality and Individual Differences, 116,* 410–16.

Fisher, D. & Frey, N. (2010). *Guided instruction.* Alexandria, VA: ASCD.

Gilakjani, A. P. (2012). A match or mismatch between learning styles of the learners and teaching styles of the teachers. *International Journal Modern Education and Computer Science, 11,* 51–60.

Goddard, Y. & Goddard, R. (2019). From school leadership to differentiated instruction: A pathway to student learning in schools. *The Elementary School Journal, 120*(2), 197-219.

Hanewicz, C., Platt, A., & Arendt, A. (2017). Creating a learner-centered teaching environment using student choice assignments. *Distance Education, 38*(3), 273–87.

Honigsfeld, A. & Dunn, R. (2009). Learning-style responsive approaches for teaching typically performing and at-risk adolescents. *The Clearing House, 82*(5), 220–34.

Kolb, D. A. (1984). *Experiential learning.* Englewood Cliffs, NJ: Prentice Hall.

Kuykendall, C. (2004). *From rage to hope: Strategies for reclaiming Black and Hispanic students.* Bloomington, IN: Solution Tree.

Letele, M. J., Alexander, G., & Swanepoel, J. I. (2013). Matching/mismatching of teaching and learning styles in rural learning ecologies of Lesotho: Does it enhance academic achievement? *Journal of Human Ecology, 41*(3), 263–73.

Levy, H. M. (2008). Meeting the needs of all students through differentiated instruction: Helping every child reach and exceed standards. *The Clearing House: A Journal of Educational Strategies, Issues and Ideas, 81*(4), 161–64.

Marzano, R. (2009). The art and science of teaching/six steps to better vocabulary instruction. *Teaching for the 21st Century, 67*(1), 83–84.

Moon, T. (2005). The role of assessment in differentiation. *Theory into Practice, 44*(3), 226–33.

Reeves, D. (2001). *101 questions & answers about standards, assessment, and accountability.* Englewood, CO: Advanced Learning Press.

Prachee, S., Nambudiri, R., & Mishra, S. K. (2017). Teacher effectiveness through self-efficacy, collaboration and principal leadership. *International Journal of Educational Management, 31*(4), 505–17.

Tomlinson, C. A. & McTighe, J. (2006). *Integrating differentiated instruction and understanding by design.* Alexandria, VA: Association for Supervision and Curriculum Development.

Wrobleski, D. (1985). Finding a meaning: Reading, writing, thinking applications: double-entry notebooks, literature logs, process journals. Paper presented at the Annual Meeting of the National Council of Teachers of English Spring Conference, Houston, TX.

Chapter 5

Using Data to Inform Instruction

Instead of a national curriculum for education, what is really needed is an individual curriculum for every child.

—*Charles Handy*

In chapter 3, assessments were the focus of discussion, their types, and uses. Additionally, in chapter 4, the need for a school-based policy on assessments, with types and frequency, was further discussed. This policy should be set with the school's IT so that teachers can own the decision rather than the decision being made topdown.

Frequently, top-down decisions allow for an "us versus them" mentality, and that mentality cannot exist in a successful school. Of course, educational leaders should and will have some nonnegotiables, but decisions, as much as possible, should be made collaboratively for maximum effect. Inherently, people want to be valued and the best way to do that is to include them in the decision-making process.

Now that these practices are in place, the focus shifts to how to use that data to inform every day instruction in the classroom; assessment data is the best tool an educator can use in order to move the needle on student achievement. Teachers should use assessment data daily, no questions.

Additionally, administrators should use this data to highlight strengths and plan to remediate weaknesses found in the school's curricular program. Additionally, this practice allows administrators to know which teachers need additional support, and that support can be focused and intentional. Do not forget, however, that pre-assessments are a form of formative assessment.

PRE-ASSESSMENTS

Pre-assessments are a vital part of informed instruction and can serve as motivation for students to learn (Ainsworth, 2014; Oberg, 2010; Van Etten, Freebern, & Pressley, 1997). However, some argue that the use of pretests is impractical in that students may have little to no incentive to do their best on a pretest, thereby affecting the validity of the assessment (Bacon, 2004; Pedersen & Williams, 2004). While the first assertion can be true, so can the latter. However, what better tool does a teacher have to determine the instructional needs than a pre-assessment?

If used correctly, pre-assessments inform the teacher and the student on the following:

1. The instructional map for the unit—how much time is needed in each area. Teachers can save instructional time if students already are familiar with content.
2. The focus of the learning—the pre-assessment sets the stage for the students and informs them on the course of study.
3. The grouping needs—students can be placed in groups based on levels of knowledge so that differentiation can be more effective.

Unfortunately, the pre-assessment is often skipped in instructional design, as mentioned before, because of the perceived lack of time to incorporate such assessments. Showing teachers how to effectively use pre-assessment data can help validate the process and underscore its importance in the instructional program. Also, working with teachers, using pre-assessment data, can highlight how to effectively differentiate.

OTHER FORMATIVE ASSESSMENTS

Formative assessments should be given daily in a teacher's classroom. The data gleaned from these assessments should dictate the course of the lesson for that day as well as for the following days to come. If that data is not used in this manner, what is the purpose of the assessment? Is it just to enter a grade in the gradebook? If so, the point is entirely missed. Formative assessments that are used for the purpose of having enough grades in the gradebook highlight a teacher-centered approach to education. This is the "I taught it and it us up to you to understand it" mentality.

The paradigm shift to a student-centered approach to teaching is what is needed: "I taught it, and was I effective in doing so?" Changing the focus to teacher effectiveness is a huge, scary paradigm shift for teachers. In explaining this shift in assessment data to teachers, the comparison can be drawn to training a high jumper to compete as a part of a team.

Educators place the high bar at the desired height a student must clear the bar when jumping to be successful in the classroom. They do this with the grading system. A student athlete, however, is not expected to jump the hurdle or clear the bar without training. Teachers can't just say, "Jump! If you clear the bar, you pass!" Students, parents, nor teachers would expect this kind of system.

We must train the students to incrementally improve their jumping ability through practice. That is the function of formative assessments—the practice. Coaches watch athletes' techniques and provide feedback and assistance, often changing techniques, to improve skills. If coaches simply told athletes to practice without constructive feedback and training, very few athletes would experience the same level of success. Teachers are the same in this respect.

In order for formative assessments to be effective, the criteria for success has to be understood by the students as well as the teacher. Remember, the formative assessments need to be aligned to the cognitive level of the standard. Look at several types of formative assessments and student-centered criteria for success in table 5.1.

Though there are a plethora of types of formative assessments and certainly more than listed above, the point is that none of the criterion listed includes completion or rote memorization of facts. In a recent discussion, a math teacher expressed that he checked homework for completion and then he went over the work with the students. He wanted to know if that was sufficient for the purposes of a formative assessment. The question remained how he knew that all students in his class understood the mathematical processes and how to use them if he only checked for completion.

Students are not always willing to tell you they do not understand for fear of failure and embarrassment (Beiter et al., 2015; Giel et al., 2019), and teachers should understand what students know and do not know prior to a summative assessment. If teachers use check for completion as grading

Table 5.1 Formative Assessment Types

Formative Assessment	Criteria
Homework	Checked for accuracy
In-class Discussion	Checked for depth of understanding
Interactive Notebook Entries	Checked for depth of understanding
Quiz	Checked for understanding and application
Exit Tickets	Checked for understanding
Post Cards	Checked for depth of understanding
Venn Diagrams	Checked for depth of understanding

criteria for homework and classwork, they will never know about which topics students truly need help. This teacher felt that when he went over the work with the students, that was sufficient to gauge understanding. Of course, this assumption was challenged through the course of the conversation.

The discussion then turned to how teachers handle the demands of grading. This is a fair topic of consideration because teachers certainly have their hands full and have limited time. However, there are ways to handle grading overloads while still obtaining useful data on formative assessments. For this math teacher, the suggestion was made to select one of each type of problem to grade for accuracy and understanding. The teacher may only check a few problems for understanding, but that practice gives more data to continue instruction.

The same can be true for any discipline. For example, if an English teacher was focusing on persuasive writing and assigned a one-page essay for homework, the teacher could grade that essay quickly based on the elements of persuasion for which the teacher was specifically looking. Meaning, the grading procedures would be focused on the lesson, not on information yet to be presented.

Students should have a chance to revise and edit for grammar and spelling before a final submission anyway. Student effort increases when they know someone is looking at their work, just as teachers do. This commonsense phenomenon was named the Hawthorne Effect based on studies conducted in the 1920s industrial setting (Diaper, 1990). Think about the behavior of students when the principal walks in the classroom; students behave differently because the principal is present.

That brings up another point—not only do teachers need that data to inform daily instruction, they must also remember to value student efforts. One must remember that the same thing that is said for teachers is true for students. If teachers have to write lesson plans, then administrators better read them to show they value the teachers' efforts. If students are asked to do homework, then teachers better grade it to show value for their efforts. If teachers do not care, students will not care; if administrators don't care, teachers will not care. Students should never be held to a higher standard than the adults.

Teachers are not the only ones who should be using formative assessment data: students should use the data as well. The goal is to develop metacognitive skills in students so that they can monitor their own learning and adjust when needed. Formative assessment data allows students to do just that, monitor their learning (Black, 2007; Brookhart, 2017; Wiggins, 2012). If a student is not performing well, the formative assessments will highlight areas of needed additional study and possibly a need for a different approach. Students then can directly own and impact their own education.

Go back to the high-jump analogy for a minute. Students who do not have the benefit of quality formative assessment data are left to rely on their God-given talents. Most people would not fare well in that system at all, as not everyone possesses strong athletic abilities. Training and coaching are needed in both cases.

Can teachers use quick checks as formative assessments? Absolutely, teachers can utilize a quick check or online poll to determine students' basic understandings; however, this type of formative assessment is not cognitively aligned and, therefore, will not afford the teacher the opportunity to gauge effectiveness of teaching. These types of assessments give the teacher just enough information to know if the teacher can dive in at the desired cognitive level: Do students have a basic understanding of concepts before a deep dive? Quick checks include assessments like the following:

1. Thumbs Up/Thumbs Down
2. Homework Checked for Completion
3. Definitions Activity
4. Five Words to Describe Activity
5. Study Guide
6. Twitter Post on "What I Learned Today"
7. Clickers
8. Kahoot!

So, how do administrators and teachers reconcile a number of required formative assessments for the school policy if these assessments are to be given daily, sometimes more than one in a grade period? The gradebook formative assessments should be the cognitively aligned assessments, not the quick checks. Premature grade conflation can happen otherwise, and unfortunately, this happens too often.

Think about the scenario in which a teacher only gives completion-type and quick check formative assessments because, let's face it, these types of assessments are easier to grade and are less time consuming. This teacher thinks the class has grasped the material and is ready for the summative assessment. After all, grades have been good, and engagement is high based on completion rates. Let's not forget with the advent of technology, parents can see these same grades as well.

However, when the teacher gives the summative assessment, students fail miserably. What is the typical teacher's response? Students did not study or did not do their homework are typical responses. However, sometimes you get "I don't know what happened" as a response. However, in this scenario, the teacher did not just not know what happened on the test, but the teacher did not know what was happening all through the unit.

What are the parents' responses to the drastic drop in grades? Normally, parent responses equate to some value judgment about the teacher's ability and professionalism. Certainly, educators want to avoid negative parent perceptions at all cost because students will use those perceptions as excuses for lack of performance rather than reflect on their own learning.

SUMMATIVE ASSESSMENTS

Summative assessments are given at the end of a unit of study and are considered terminal assessments. Teachers often view the summative assessment as unit assessments which signal the start of new material; however, summative assessments are really formative assessments if used correctly. The only true summative assessment, as stated earlier, should be the final exam. In this scenario, assessments are used for learning rather than a measure of learning.

Remember, not all students learn at the same rate. Shouldn't students be given the opportunity to demonstrate mastery at different intervals if the true goal is learning? For the purposes of this section, however, the term "formative assessment" is interchangeable with unit assessment.

From an administrative perspective, teachers should use formative assessment data to inform daily instruction. Summative assessment data should also be used to inform remediation needs. In order for useful information to be gleaned from these summative assessments, they must be formatted in such a way to provide standards-based information. Follow the logic. A teacher reports grades on a test and a class average for a unit. Students are given grades such as 81, 94, 79, and so on. All students see in this case is that they passed the test. All teachers see is the class average.

Now, if those tests were labeled by standard/indicator, teachers and students can see what standards were mastered and which students need additional support with specific standards. See example 5.2. Each question on the assessment needs to be labeled by standard. Following this guideline produces useful guidance and information for the teacher, student, and administrator.

Several items need to be addressed by administration with teachers in order for this system to work:

1. Collaborative determination of mastery levels—the teachers and administration need to collectively decide what is deemed as mastery of learning for standards. Is it 70 percent or 80 percent? Once this is determined, the number of assessment items per standard/indicator needs to be set. Obviously, two questions, like in the example mentioned earlier, for an indicator is not sufficient.
2. Summative assessments need to be analyzed for *mastery by standard.*

Example 5.2   Biology Test

Biology 1: Cells Unit Test

H.B.2B.3

  1. In which ways are virus cells dependent on living cells?

    a. Reproduction

    b. Energy

    c. Food

    d. a and b, but not c

  2. How are virus cells different than living cells?

    a. Viral cells contain RNA and living cells contain DNA.

    b. Viral cells use hosts' energy whereas living cells produce their own energy.

    c. Viral cells are much larger than living cells.

    d. All of the above

---

3. If mastery is set at 80 percent, then a minimum of five questions per indicator is sufficient. Students can miss one question for that standard/indicator and still be deemed proficient (4/5).

4. Students need to help analyze their own results to determine mastery and experience success. This enables students to own their learning: they see in what areas they need remediation help.

The benefits of this type of system are multiple. Teachers see on what topics they were most effective and in which areas they may need help. From this type of analyses, teachers can discuss best practices in teaching with their colleagues. Imagine one teacher is very successful with a standard while another is not. Conversations can be rich and meaningful if the teachers trust one another. Students understand in what areas specifically they need help as well.

Many educational institutions have redo policies for students. These policies afford students the opportunity to retake a test or quiz if they were unsuccessful. Part of the High Schools That Works initiative and Making Middle Grades Work with Southern Region Educational Board requires that schools have such a policy as part of their key practices (Schmidt-Davis & Bottoms, n.d.). However, these practices look different across schools.

Often, the teacher agrees to have some requirement for the students to fulfill prior to retaking a test, like tutoring. However, most students, the ones who really need to take advantage of the policy, don't. Honestly, most students who take advantage of this type of policy are the more grade-conscious students who want to improve their GPA's, not the ones who need to improve their grades from a failure. Why do you think that is the case?

Adults hate exercises in repetition. For example, as an administrator, imagine several different divisions in your district office ask for the same information from you. This is not uncommon. These requests take up an inordinate amount of time. You think to yourself, "Why do I have to send the same information multiple times to multiple people? Can't they just talk to each other up there?" Sound familiar? Students are no different. Retaking an entire test is repetitive.

Students don't take advantage of these redo policies because it is cumbersome to have to study for the entire unit again while the class is moving forward. Why not let students remediate the standards they did not master instead of the whole unit? With the mastery analysis by standard, students can feel success with the standards they did master and know exactly what needs further study and preparation.

In this scenario, students own their learning and are more motivated to learn. Students are not repeating their efforts, making the redo policy more manageable. Also, students can feel motivated by the fact that they may be close to mastery or that they mastered other standards and have fewer to go. Progress supports the process. Including students in the grading of mastery levels intensifies this effect. See figure 5.1 for a sample form to use with students.

Teachers who take ten minutes out of instruction to allow students to report their own mastery reap the benefits in class. Students who can see their own mastery levels can celebrate successes and refocus needed efforts. The sample in figure 5.1 is an example of how to do that. Additionally, when students are asked what they did not understand, teachers are often surprised by the responses. Students will never disappoint in telling you if questions were misworded or the information was never taught.

Student Name_____	Unit_____	
Standard 1.1 _____ /5	_____ %	
Standard 3.2 _____ /5	_____ %	
Standard 3.3 _____ /5	_____ %	
Standard 4.5 _____ /5	_____ %	
I MASTERED STANDARDS:		
I NEED FURTHER REVIEW ON THESE STANDARDS:		
I DIDN'T UNDERSTAND:		

Figure 5.1   **Student Grading of Mastery.**

However, the misunderstanding could have come from a confusing question, something said during instruction, or something from the student's background schemata. Confusion is inevitable and knowing from where the confusion originates is the only way to clarify and clear the misunderstanding. In this scenario, asking the question affords the teacher the opportunity to clear up misunderstanding that may not take more instructional time.

Though summative assessment data is not the only data that should be utilized by administrators, it certainly is a key piece of data that lets the administrator know exactly where teachers and students are in the learning of the curriculum as close to real time as possible. Discussion of the use of this data will continue in the section on data meetings. Data, if used correctly, becomes data for learning, not an evaluation of student learning or teacher success.

OBSERVATION DATA

Some of the most often overlooked data useful to administrators is observation data. Admittedly, observations provide a brief snapshot of what is happening in classrooms. However, this information is quite useful if it is organized well. Observations should also have a focus. Often times, administrators are fulfilling a district requirement of a specified number of observations a week, walkthrough and formal observations. Both types of observations should be viewed as qualitative and/or quantitative measures.

Quantitative Observations

When conducting walkthrough observations, it is best to make sure that a focus is provided for that observation period. Principals should provide that focus for the assistant principals so that the data for the week can be analyzed as a team. Teachers should know what the varied foci will be for observations, but not necessarily for each week. For example, one week's focus might be student engagement. The next week's focus might be cognitive level of instructional activities. Another week's focus might be writing activities. The observation forms should reflect the priorities and vision of the leadership.

By making sure that the observation form represents the instructional priorities, teachers and assistant principals understand more clearly the instructional expectations. Each week, the focus of the walkthrough observations can be tabulated to give the principal valuable information on the status of the instructional program. All observation information should be quantifiable in order to provide data that is usable in a timely manner.

For example, one week's quantitative data may show that only fifteen of fifty teachers utilized active student engagement activities whereas the remaining thirty-five teachers were utilizing passive engagement instructional activities. If this pattern continues, some work is needed. See figure 5.2 for an example of an observation quantifiable chart.

This quantification through walkthrough observations can guide a professional development plan for a school. Of course, patterns do need to emerge. Because walkthrough observations are only a snapshot, principals need to make sure that a pattern of behavior exists before implementing some professional development program. The data from these observations should be shared with the Leadership Team and teachers. In doing so, teachers become more aware of their strategies and may adjust before a true pattern emerges.

Qualitative Observations

Qualitative observations are more time consuming, but can still demonstrate patterns of strength and weakness in a building. These more formal observations should last at least 20–30 minutes, and oftentimes a full class period. The observer should script the observation. Again, the focus should be provided for the observation in advance of the classroom observation.

This type of observation is when the observer can notate the types and levels of questions asked in a classroom, the ability of the teacher to draw the answers from students and allow for appropriate wait time, the cross-section

Informal Observation Data
August 22- Sept. 6

Focus	Observations	Needs
State Standards Displayed and Referenced throughout	8	1
Student Demonstration of Mastery	6	3
Expectations are clear and high	7	2
Meaningful and relevant content organization	9	0
Consistent reinforcement and rewards	8	1
Explicit Examples, Illustrations, etc. for new concepts	5	4
Teacher Modeling	5	4
Logical sequencing	8	1
Close Reading	6	3
Writing Across the Curriculum	7	2

Figure 5.2 Observation Quantification Chart.

of students engaged in the lesson, and so on. The focus, again, should be aligned to the instructional priorities of the school and the state evaluation system.

At the end of the observation, the observer should then reflect on the focus of the observations for the week and be able to discuss findings with the administrative team. This information is then used to help determine teacher goals, professional development needs, and additional supports for teachers. Of course, patterns should emerge with teachers prior to establishing any of these supports. Preemptive professional development for all teachers can serve to alienate teachers when they feel it is unnecessary of a waste of time.

Furthermore, best practices can be identified in these observations. Teachers provide the best professional development to other teachers, and teachers are more often respected than an outside agency or consultant. Simply, the best resources can be found in your own building. If a teacher is a champion at questioning techniques that push students to deeper levels of thinking, then that teacher should be tapped to provide professional development for other teachers. The same can be said for any instructional priority.

By seeking best practices in your building, you are not only providing a valuable service to other teachers, but you are also affirming teachers. They feel valued in this process, which impacts teacher morale. This certainly is a win-win scenario. Only through focused observations can you find these gems, celebrate teachers, and provide needed support to others. Again, the formal observation forms need to reflect the instructional priorities for the school.

LOCUS OF FOCUS

As discussed, each type of observation should have a focus. This focus prevents administrators from looking for the simple things in a classroom like standards posted on the board and rules posted in the room versus transitions, student engagement, and cognitive demand. Too often, administrators feel pressured to meet an observation quota and may resort to the less important factors in a classroom for expediency. However, providing a weekly focus also makes the observation expedient and meaningful.

The focus should shift multiple times in a year, based on the instructional priorities set at the beginning of the school year. These priorities should be set with the Leadership Team so that everyone understands what administrators are looking for in the classroom and why. If teachers understand expectations, they will more than likely demonstrate success. The same is said for students. If teachers share this information with students, what is expected of them in the course of a class, then they, too, will most often rise to the occasion.

The results of the observations, again, should be shared for transparency as well as to demonstrate the need for professional developments. If teachers understand the "why," then they will own the instructional changes needed. Teachers want to perform well for the sake of their students, as they want their students to succeed. Teachers do not want to feel scrutinized or observed with no feedback given. This practice does not lend itself to professional growth.

However, teachers often do not know what they need at times. Data tells the story, and data from observations paints the picture. Additionally, reporting school data demonstrates that teachers are not alone in their struggles, and no one person is singled out. The school owns the problem, not people. This type of practice is far less threatening.

DATA MEETINGS

Data meetings give a principal the best picture of student achievement progressions in a school. This is a strong progress monitoring tool for administrators that is often underutilized because of the time these meetings take. Not only do these meetings require administrative time, but the time teachers need to prepare for the meetings can be a deterrent for some. However, data meetings are the best administrative and teacher time spent if the goal is to move the needle on student achievement. These meetings should be frequent and meaningful.

In order to have successful data meetings, of course, teachers need to understand the expectations first. They need to know what to bring to the meeting and what to be prepared to discuss. Now, if summative assessments are analyzed by standard, as mentioned earlier, logic dictates this data would be the focus of the meetings. For example, a monthly data meeting with all math teachers in which standards proficiency is discussed will illuminate instructional strengths, instructional weaknesses, as well as issues with the curricula.

Imagine all math teachers sitting in a room discussing proficiency rates by standard. Patterns will definitely emerge, and these patterns can cross subject areas as well. Imagine a high school math data meeting where Algebra 1, Algebra 2, and Pre-Calculus, and Calculus teachers are all in the room discussing the struggles students had with the prior unit. If the principal is listening closely, the principal will detect patterns. These patterns may be holes in the curriculum or may represent the need for additional focus in the courses.

For example, one science meeting can identify issues, such as transfer of energy across all science courses. The standards based on transfer of energy should then become a focus for every science class. Facilitating these conversations strengthens the entire science curriculum in a school. In doing so, students will be more prepared for the next science class they take, whether it is biology, chemistry, or physics.

In an English meeting, understanding elements of persuasion may emerge as a weakness. Of course, this information will never come to light without departmental data meetings and the information gleaned is most invaluable for administrators and teachers. Again, the English curriculum is strengthened across all grade levels as a result of these types of meetings.

However, in order for these meetings to be most effective, teachers need to feel safe sharing their data. These summative assessments, that should be viewed as formative assessments, should not be used to evaluate a teacher. Teachers should not be evaluated on formative data ever. They should be evaluated on what they do with the data. If data meetings show patterns and weaknesses, teachers need to understand that it is imperative that they are willing to back up and reteach if necessary. The expectation that students will score phenomenally well all of the time is unrealistic.

Therefore, teachers need to feel safe saying they taught the material and students did not learn it well. Teachers can share best practices in these meetings as well. Where one teacher might have struggled with a standard, another might have experienced great success. As a result, teachers learn from one another and are given more tools in their tool belts without judgment.

It is important that teachers understand that while students may have a redo policy, teachers need to have one, too. For example, if a good percentage of a class did not perform well on a standard, the teacher needs a redo. Teachers need to feel secure in admitting this to their peers and their principal. This is normal because teachers cannot expect to be perfect every day. However, examining teacher effectiveness can be scary for teachers if they do not trust their administration.

A principal, in conjunction with the Leadership Team, needs to establish the teacher redo policy along with the student redo policy. Remember, the aim is student learning. For example, if, say, 40 percent of a class or more did not perform well on a standard, the teacher has to redo. If, say, 30 percent of students did not perform well while 70 percent did perform well, then that 30 percent of students need a redo, not the teacher.

Of course, a Leadership Team needs to feel good about the percentages set in a school policy as well as what a student redo means. Additionally, the principal needs to keep the focus on student learning at all times. See figures 5.3 and 5.4 for different reporting methods. Each method provides some valuable information.

Upon reviewing this standard report, an English teacher can easily see that she was ineffective in teaching two standards, character and tone/mood. Because a majority of students were not successful on these standards across

Standard		Block 1		Block 2		Block 3		Block 4	
1.1 Inference	96%	25	100%	20	95%	17	94%	19	95%
1.2 POV	75%	14	96%	12	57%	15	83%	13	66%
1.4 Character	64%	16	64%	10	48%	12	67%	15	75%
1.4 Conflict	88%	25	100%	18	86%	16	89%	15	75%
1.5 F/F	73%	24	96%	15	71%	11	61%	13	65%
1.5 Symbolism	90%	25	100%	18	86%	15	83%	18	90%
1.5 Tone/Mood	53%	17	68%	10	48%	12	56%	8	40%
3.1 Context Clues	86%	25	100%	18	86%	14	78%	16	80%
# Tested		25		21		10		20	

Figure 5.3   Sample Standards Proficiency Report.

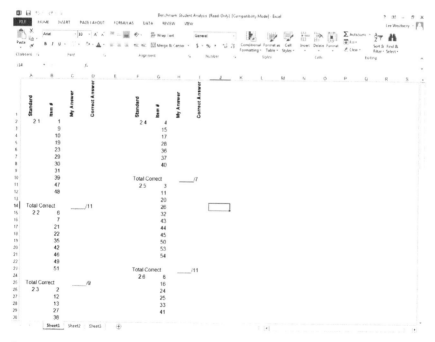

Figure 5.4   Sample Standard Report.

classes, the teacher need to first look at the assessment to determine if there was an issue with the assessment. If the assessment is aligned, then the teacher may need to reteach and reassess these standards.

If different classes show different results, the teacher may want to examine the reading levels of the students in the class to determine if the material was accessible to the students. Additionally, the teacher may have changed how she taught a standard, or the teacher may not have differentiated enough for the students. In either case, the teacher may want a redo and reteach the material.

In the example mentioned earlier, each indicator is separated by the questions that address the indicator. This analysis makes it easy for a teacher to see if the questions themselves are problematic. What if students understand a portion of the standard, but not the entire standard. By providing an item analysis with questions, teachers can determine precisely what students may not understand. This analysis allows for truly focused remediation as well.

SYSTEMS PERSPECTIVE

In order to develop a systems perspective on using data to inform instruction, a principal, alongside a school Leadership Team, needs to establish expectations for assessments (frequency and type), observations, and data meetings. All of the data derived from assessments will be used in data meetings, and observation data will provide another lens from which to see the instructional function of the school.

The first step is to establish an assessment policy in the school. How many summative assessments are required each unit? Every four weeks? How many formative assessments should be included each week? How many aligned formative assessments for each portion of instruction? These grades will be seen by students and parents alike, so ensuring the quality of assessments is imperative. Therefore, the suggestion that assessments should be submitted with lesson plans is not ridiculous, as was discussed in the chapter on assessments.

The second step is to establish proficiency rates for standards in order to determine mastery. This should be done with the Leadership Team as well. Will a student have to answer 75 percent, or three out of four questions per standard, correctly to be deemed proficient? With an 80 percent proficiency rate, will a student have to answer four out of five correctly for each standard? Once established, then teachers will know how many questions per standard must be present and labeled on summative assessments.

The third step is to set redo policies for the school, both student and teacher redo's. The Leadership Team must own these policies in order for them to be effective. The teacher who tells the student to jump, as discussed in the high-jump analogy, will not appreciate a teacher redo policy. Students also need to understand their responsibilities for redo. Again, if sounds are not required to redo an entire unit, just standards they did not master, they are more apt to take advantage of the policy, especially if they are engaged in the scoring of mastery.

The fourth step is to establish expectations for data meetings (frequency, dates and times, information required, discussion parameters). Again, it cannot be stressed enough that teachers need to feel safe in these meetings. The agendas for these meetings should include the following: proficiency rates by standards, best practices revealed, redo statistics, and patterns that emerge. If this is the focus of the meetings rather than student behaviors and other obstacles to learning, the data meetings can be quite effective.

In fact, the data meetings can provide great professional development for teachers while allowing teachers to own the instructional program of the school. Teachers will be motivated to redo and learn from one another all while refocusing curriculum where it is needed. An additional positive outcome is that the principal will know where professional development needs exist as well as where to expend school funds. Teachers will tell the principal what they need specifically in teaching standards during these meetings. So, data meetings also provide focus to a school's finance practices.

The fifth step is to provide focus for observations, both quantitative and qualitative observations. This focus will also provide useful data for the principal and Leadership Team. When reviewing data in data meetings, the principal will also think about the observation data shared by the administrative team. The two are definitely connected, no doubt. Again, focus is provided for professional development needs and spending practices.

SUMMARY

Using data to inform instruction is one of the most important tasks in a school, from both the teacher perspective and the principal perspective. Teachers should use formative assessment data continually to inform their daily instruction. Summative assessment data should be viewed as formative and also used to inform instruction. Principals should use summative assessment data along with observation data, both qualitative and quantitative, in order to paint a full picture of the instructional program in the school.

Observations should also have a focus based on the instructional priorities of the school, and teachers should know the instructional priorities. The focus of the observations should rotate and change in order to determine patterns of behavior in the school. Without this type of practice, observations can only serve to highlight an ill-prepared teacher or a superb teacher, but the real deficiencies among a staff may never surface.

Of course, all collective data should be shared with the staff. Data meetings should be held at regular intervals, and teachers need to understand the expectations for the meetings. Teachers should feel safe to share successes and failures as well as feel comfortable learning from one another. The agendas for the meetings set the stage for effective discourse.

In order to develop a systems perspective, certain school policies need to be established first: assessment policies and redo policies for students and teachers. Principals will use all of the data from observations and data meetings to paint a clear picture of the instructional program in the school.

A PIECE AT A TIME

- Why are pre-assessments so important to a teacher? How can they save time?
- Which assessments are considered formative and summative?
- How should summative assessments be structured?
- How can a principal use observation data?
- What is a proficiency policy?
- What is one way to get students to own their learning?
- What is the difference between a student redo policy and a teacher redo policy?
- What should be on a data meeting agenda?
- What are the four things the principal must establish before conducting data meetings?

REFERENCES

Ainsworth, L. (2014). *Rigorous curriculum design: How to create curricular units of study that align standards, instruction, and assessment.* Englewood, CO: The Leadership and Learning Center.

Bacon, D. (2004). The contributions of reliability and pretests to effective assessment. *Practical Assessment, Research & Evaluation, 9*(3), 1–8.

Beiter, R., Nash, r., McCrady, M., Rhoades, D., Linscomb, M., Clarahan, M. & Sannut, S. (2015). The prevalance and correlates of depression, anxiety and stress in a sample of college students. *Journal of Affective Disorders, 173,* 90–96.

Black, P. (2007). Full marks for feedback. *Journal of the Institute of Educational Assessors, 2(1), Spring,* 18–21.

Brookhart, S. (2017). *How to give effective feedback to your students* (2nd ed). Alexandria, VA: ASCD.

Diaper, G. (1990). The Hawthorne effect: A fresh examination. *Educational Studies, 16*(3), 261–67.

Giel, L., Noordzij, G., Noordegraaf-Eelens, L. & Denktas, S. (2019). Fear of failure: A polynomial regression analysis of the joint impact of the perceived learning environment and personal achievement goal orientation. *Anxiety, Stress & Coping, 33*(2), 123–39.

Oberg, C. (2010). Guiding classroom instruction through performance assessment. *Journal of Case Studies in Accreditation and Assessment, 1,* 1–11.

Pedersen, S. & Williams, D. (2004). A comparison of assessment practices and their effects on learning and motivation in a student-centered learning environment. *Journal of Educational Multimedia and Hypermedia, 13*(3), 283–306.

Schmidt-Davis, J. & Bottoms, G. (n.d.). *Turnaround high school principals: Recruit, prepare and empower leaders of change.* Atlanta Georgia: SREB.

Van Etten, S., Freebern, G., & Pressley, M. (1997). College students' beliefs about exam preparation. *Contemporary Educational Psychology, 22,* 192–212.

Wiggins, G. (2012). Seven keys to effective feedback. *Educational Leadership, 70*(1), 10–16.

Chapter 6

Focused Remediation

Facts do not cease to exist because they are ignored.

—*Aldous Huxley*

Remediation programs are not new to schools. Most schools have remedial classes, or classes that are designed to help the struggling learner, in which the curriculum is taught at a slower pace. Tutoring programs also exist to provide remediation for students who struggle. Additionally, the aforementioned "redo policy" is a form of remediation for students to demonstrate mastery of learning. These are just a few examples of remediation programs. However, what is often missing from schools is a remediation plan that addresses all three levels of learners from the beginning.

THREE LEVELS OF LEARNERS

In every class, three levels of learners exist. It does not matter if the class is a remedial class or an Advanced Placement (AP) class. There are those students who will understand and excel no matter what the teacher does (top level), those that are in the middle who rely on teacher instruction (middle level), and those who will struggle continuously (lower level). Even in an AP class, those same three levels of learners exist.

Traditionally, teachers teach to the middle level because that is the majority composition of a class. Think of the Bell Curve. The majority of scores lie within the second and third quartile, the middle. Plans may exist for the struggling student after they have experienced failed attempts at mastery, but this is often late in the process and is rarely taken advantage of. Honestly, teachers teach to a majority which is supposed to be representative of the grade-level classroom.

Very rarely, however, do plans exist for the top level of the class, or those above grade level, to enrich and extend learning. All three levels of learners require planning in advance of instruction in order for instruction to operate smoothly with no loss of instructional time. In order to do this, teachers have to know who they have in their classrooms before the students take a seat on the first day.

Each lesson should be planned with all three levels of learners in advance. This cannot be stressed enough. How do teachers do this? First, teachers must examine the data on their students through the schools' data management systems. Each school has some system of data that shows the achievement level of students since entering a school system. Even if the data is not available through technology, the data can be found in student files.

Whether the data is terminal data such as state testing data or progress monitoring data, such as Measures of Academic Achievement, which measures what students know and what they are ready to learn next, (NWEA, 2019) or Reading Inventories, which provide a growth assessment (Houghton Mifflin Harcourt, 2019), it is important to examine prior to planning instruction. Without this information, teachers are, again, planning for the middle. Of upmost importance is for a teacher to know the reading levels of their students.

Reading levels determine the ease of access to the curriculum. Very rarely is a class comprised of students all on the same reading level. If the world were that simple! Look at the table 6.1 for a typical class composition of reading levels. The Lexile Levels listed are measures of a student's reading comprehension at the difficulty level of text. This measure approximates the readers ability to comprehend material within complex text (MetaMetrics, 2019). Lexile levels are being utilized on national levels at this time.

Table 6.1   Typical Class with Lexile Scores

Student	Lexile Level
Student 1	637
Student 2	742
Student 3	1,250
Student 4	1,000
Student 5	1,300
Student 6	920
Student 7	955
Student 8	800
Student 9	1,120
Student 10	674
Student 11	1,275
Student 12	875

This measure is important to understand when considering textbooks and assigned reading materials that students will have to encounter. If the text is not accessible to the student due to lower Lexile abilities, the teacher will have to plan in advance for that student or the student will no doubt experience failure. Too often, this is exactly what happens. Imagine being the student who is expected to read and learn but cannot comprehend the text. How frustrating that must be. Let's assume that the rather small class above in table 6.1 represents a typical sixth-grade classroom.

The teacher will have to organize the Lexile scores in numerical ascending order in order to see the levels clearly. According to MetaMetrics, the company that created Lexile measures based on years of research (2019), the typical band for a sixth-grade student mid-year ranges from 855 Lexile to 1165 Lexile. This band represents the bottom 25 percent to the top 75 percent of students nationally. So, when examining the table 6.1, the class can be divided into the three levels of learners represented in the class.

What are the advantages of knowing these data sets in advance? Typically, teachers figure out who is going to struggle in their classes pretty quickly. These children historically have demonstrated struggle throughout their academic careers. However, teachers often do not know why the struggle exists and often attribute the apathy to attitude. As struggling students get older and have more experience in the educational system, they tend to accept and even expect failure. Students who fear failure are less threatened by putting in little effort and failing than putting in a lot of effort and failing (Covington, 1985). In essence, there is not much to lose.

Teachers see the behaviors in students and the lack of interest, but often do not understand that "many classrooms are failure-oriented" (Covington, 1985, p. 390), and educators are guilty of setting these students up for failure without even knowing it. Of course, that would never be a teacher's aim, but it happens nonetheless.

From analyzing data on students prior to them starting the class, a teacher can determine who will struggle and plan for those students in advance. For example, table 6.2 distinguishes the three levels of learners found in this classroom, divided by approximate grade-level comprehension skills. Teachers can use this information to differentiate strategies, materials, groups, and so on. Options are available once one recognizes the variance.

Teachers, after understanding the abilities of their students, can then plan for the learners in advance. What materials will be used so the lower level of students can understand the instructional material? How will grouping be used in the classroom? How will the teacher enrich and extend the highest level of learner in the classroom? How will the teacher focus on growth for all three levels and monitor that growth?

Table 6.2   Three Levels of Learners in a Typical Sixth-Grade Classroom

Student	Lexile	Approximate Grade—Level Comprehension	Level
Student 1	637	3–4	1
Student 10	674	3–4	1
Student 2	742	4	1
Student 8	800	4–5	1
Student 12	875	4–5	1
Student 6	920	5–6	2
Student 7	955	5–6	2
Student 4	1,000	6–7	2
Student 9	1,120	7–8	2
Student 3	1,250	9	3
Student 11	1,275	9–11	3
Student 5	1,300	9–11	3

The highest level of learner is often overlooked because they tend to complete the work and excel. Additionally, these students are often not the behavior problem in a classroom, which often offers a reprise for the teachers. Therefore, the teacher feels success as the students succeed on grade-level materials. However, what happens to advanced students who are not accelerated beyond the average ability of the classroom? Human nature will prevail, unfortunately.

ENRICHMENT NEEDED

Students who are not engaged to achieve at higher levels often can become less motivated (Caraway, Tucker, Reinke & Hall, 2003; Glick et al., 2019). These students have the tendency to regress to the norm of the class, the middle level. Students should grow at least a year every year, and this requires advance planning on the teacher's part to extend the higher-level students in order for them to achieve their full potential. Therefore, differentiated materials and assignments need to be created for all levels of children in order to maximize student achievement.

Understanding the three levels of students in advance also allows teachers to effectively design groups in the classroom. Grouping within a classroom has proven to have positive effects on student achievement (Slavin & Karweit, 1984; Thompson, 1974). Think about grouping techniques that are often used and how they can change depending on the assignment. Lower-level students can be motivated by working with students with higher Lexile ranges once material is comprehended (Azmitia, 1988; Hooper & Hannafin, 1988).

Teachers can also put students together in groups so that the teacher can spend more time with the students who need it most, all while checking in on the other groups. The beauty of this grouping is that members of all three groups may rotate in and out of the group that needs more assistance, depending on the instructional demands of the lessons. Grouping within a classroom has positive effects on student achievement.

The third-level students need assignments that will challenge their thinking as well. These grouping techniques allow for differentiation of instruction in the classroom, which teachers often find most challenging. Again, students from other groups may rotate in and out of the challenging assignments, depending on the interest and motivation created by the designed lessons. In essence, students will never know to which group they belong, and they shouldn't (Palacios et al., 2019).

In order to feel success and pride, students should not feel a stigma associated with the three levels. No longer do the bluebirds and blackbirds exist. Only the teacher will know who belongs to which group, and the teacher can plan to address the needs of all students in advance. In doing so, all students can feel success in the classroom, which is the most motivating factor for all.

Classroom Practice

In the previous chapter on assessment, standard-specific analysis was discussed and deemed powerful, especially when students help determine with which standards they need additional help. Couple that analysis with pre-planned instructional materials and strategies to meet the needs of the three levels of learners in the classroom, and remediation takes on a laser focus. In this scenario, the teacher knows exactly what each student needs to be successful and master the standards. Even better, the students know exactly what they need as well.

Developing a system within the classroom in which students know the process and procedures for remediation is important and often the most difficult for teachers to navigate. This requires up-front planning by the teacher, but saves so much time in the long run. For example, after an analysis of an assessment, if a student knows he needs remediation on two standards, that student should know where to go to get the needed materials and assistance as well as the timeline to complete the remediation prior to a reassessment on those specific standards. The reassessment is critical, and remember that no one likes an exercise in redundancy.

With proper grouping and cognitively aligned formative assessments, the hope is fewer students will need this remediation. However, the remediation that is provided needs to be timely and focused. Think of a potential classroom design as seen in figure 6.1. The stations allow for rotation of mastery, enrichment, and remediation. Timelines are given for completion by the teacher, but students rotate in and out of stations and grouping that maximizes

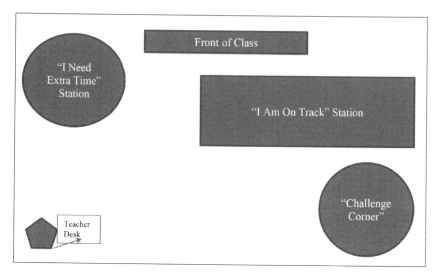

Figure 6.1   Classroom Setup for Differentiation.

their chances for mastery before moving on. Even if the teacher has to move on to the next unit, remediation is still a possibility.

In this set up, students do not feel stigmatized and can work with other students instead of feeling isolated in their academics. Of course, this classroom design does not have to be used every day. Teachers can give whole-class instruction, modeling, and guided practice in a traditional setting and then break to this design when independent work is assigned or when coming close to ending a unit. Students can feel free to move from one station to the next when they feel they have mastered the standards being addressed. This fluidity allows for the progression of learning for all students.

Some students may never get to the Challenge Corner, and that is ok. However, all students should move through to the "I Am On Track" Station, which indicates comprehension. The major differences will come from the differentiation of materials for each station. With the "I Need Extra Time" Station, the varied levels of materials on the standards afford the lower Lexile student to comprehend the material. That basic comprehension then allows them to understand the task at hand when the student moves to the "I Am On Track" Station. The higher-level Lexile student should end up in the "Challenge Corner" and should be pushed to do so.

What teachers will find in this scenario is that the middle-level students will find themselves in the "Challenge Corner" more often, which extends their learning along with the higher Lexile student. The lower Lexile students will find themselves successful in the "I Am On Track" Station and maybe even make it to the "Challenge Corner." This set up allows for maximum student engagement and learning opportunities, despite levels, as well as motivation to learn. Of course, there are other class designs that can assist in the same remediation endeavors.

Forms

As an administrator, you should help guide teachers in this practice. The planning that is required can be difficult for teachers to grasp, in that many teachers do not plan that far ahead. In order to help facilitate this process, administrators can assist with a simple form that teachers fill out when unit planning. This form enables teachers to think far ahead and informs the administration on what the instruction will look like in the classroom. See figure 6.2 for a sample form.

This form also informs administration on what to expect during classroom observations as well as helps facilitate those data conversations. Teachers can explain the remediation provided and reassessment results with ease. Because the classroom system then allows for immediate remediation, the reassessment results are often readily available for the data conversations. This allows administration to truly see patterns of instructional weakness and strength within the building.

Notice that the form asks for class period or block. Even if the teacher teaches two or three of the same classes, this form should be completed for each class. Most teachers who are assigned to teach say two sections of English 1 plan their lessons for both classes alike. How much different can the lessons be? However, one must ask if that teacher teaches both classes the same way using the same strategies and materials, and if the teacher meets the needs of all students? Take a look at two ninth-grade classes worth of data in table 6.3 before you answer that question.

MULTIPLE CLASSES

Certainly, the teacher cannot assume to teach the two classes in the same manner with the differences in the students represented. The second period class contains students who need more enrichment, which will have to become part of the regular classroom instruction. The first class of students needs more differentiated material so that the curriculum is accessible based on the Lexile scores of the class. As such, the teacher will need to develop strong, varying remediation materials for the first class all the while planning for the few students who are at or near grade level in that class.

Consequently, the daily classroom instruction should look somewhat different between the two classes even though the students are learning the same

Teacher Name_____   Class_____
                                       Period (Block) _____
Standards: _____
Students are Expected To:

The 3 Levels of Learners in My Classroom:

Level 1 Range: _____

┌──┐
│   │
│   │
└──┘

Level 2 Range: _____

┌──┐
│   │
│   │
│   │
└──┘

Level 3 Range: _____

┌──┐
│   │
│   │
│   │
└──┘

My Plans for Remediation:

┌──┐
│   │
│   │
└──┘

My Plans for Enrichment:

┌──┐
│   │
│   │
│   │
└──┘

Figure 6.2   Remediation and Enrichment Form.

standards. The same curriculum still needs to be taught, as the standards are the same. However, students are not the same; therefore, teachers must adjust strategies and materials to meet the needs of the students.

Administrators, when conducting observations, should look for varied instructional strategies and even materials based on the needs of the students. Pacing should be similar between classes, as too often the students are left

Table 6.3   Two Classroom Data Sets

Student	Lexile	Approximate Grade Level
First Period English 1		
Student 1	875	5
Student 2	900	6
Student 3	900	6
Student 4	930	6
Student 5	975	7
Student 6	1,000	7
Student 7	1,020	7
Student 8	1,100	8
Student 9	1,170	8
Student 10	1,250	9
Second Period English 1		
Student 1	1,000	7
Student 2	1,010	7
Student 3	1,030	7
Student 4	1,120	9
Student 5	1,150	9
Student 6	1,200	9
Student 7	1,250	9
Student 8	1,350	11/12
Student 9	1,375	11/12
Student 10	1,410	11/12

to feel that they cannot perform well so they choose not to perform at all, as a self-fulfilling prophecy (Brophy, 1983). This type of differentiation eliminates some obstacles for students.

SYSTEMS PERSPECTIVE

In order for administrators to support teachers in this differentiating endeavor with focused remediation, of course, a principal cannot assume that a teacher knows inherently how to perform this instructional juggling act. Teachers need professional development before embarking on a new instructional path, and principals should be a part of that development. Like any curricular issue, the process begins with education and continues through progress monitoring. See figure 6.3 for a model.

Principals need to understand that this type of change is a process, and change is difficult. Therefore, the principal will need to provide supportive feedback for teachers to remain motivated to see the results. The vast majority of teachers want their students to be successful, and once teachers see the results, the results serve as additional motivation. Continual fine tuning of professional development, process, and feedback is necessary to make the change stick.

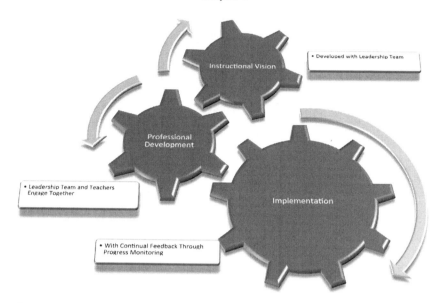

Figure 6.3   Process of Curricular Change.

Think about a child who gets braces. Once the braces are removed after an extended period of time (professional development and implementation), that same child has to wear a retainer for years in order for the change in the position of teeth to become permanent (continued professional development and progress monitoring). If the child does not wear the retainer regularly, the teeth shift back to their original position. The same is true with any change. A system of progress monitoring through lesson plans, remediation forms, observations, and continued professional development ensures that the change becomes permanent.

SUMMARY

Many schools have remediation programs that take different forms; however, most programs resemble a pin-the-tale-on-the-donkey game. Attempts are made, but the tales rarely finds its mark. Only through data analysis by indicator can educators provide focused remediation for students, giving them exactly what they need without exercises of redundancy.

Identifying the three levels of learners in each classroom is essential to providing classroom instruction and materials at the ability level of the students. Teachers must understand who is sitting in their classrooms prior to developing instructional materials. Students who are in the level three group, with the highest ability levels, are often left unchallenged because teachers typically teach to the middle and work to remediate those who struggle after experienced failure. Without addressing the needs of the higher functioning group, students tend to digress to the norm.

Identifying the three levels of learners in the classroom also allows teachers to differentiate instruction based on the needs of the student while utilizing effective grouping strategies. Up-front planning is the key to successful differentiated instruction, and there are forms that help focus the teacher on providing such instruction.

Lastly, administrators need to provide extensive professional development for teachers and engage in that same development as well as supply endless supportive feedback through the change process. In order for the change to become permanent, administrators need to have a system for change that includes instructional vision, professional development, and progress monitoring with continual feedback. This process does not stop once implementation of change begins, but remains a continual process.

A PIECE AT A TIME

- What types of classes contain three levels of learners?
- When should a teacher identify the three levels of learners in the classroom?
- How can a teacher identify the three levels of learners?
- What strategies can a teacher use to address the needs of the three levels of learners?
- Can two classes of the same subject and grade level be taught in the same way?
- How can a teacher differentiate instruction based on the three levels of learners?
- How can a principal progress monitor the differentiation and focused remediation?
- When does reassessment occur?

REFERENCES

Azmitia, M. (1988). Peer interaction and problem solving: When are two heads better than one? *Child Development, 59*(1), 87–96.

Brophy, J. E. (1983). Research on the self-fulfilling prophecy and teacher expectations. *Journal of Educational Psychology, 75*(5), 631–61.

Caraway, K., Tucker, C., Reinke, W., & Hall, C. (2003). Self-efficacy, goal orientation, and fear of failure as predictors of school engagement in high school students. *Psychology in the Schools, 40*(4), 417–27.

Covington, M. (1985). Strategic thinking and fear of failure. In J. Segal, S. Chipman, & R. Glaser (Eds.), *Thinking and learning skills vol. 1: Relating instruction to research* (Ch. 11). Hillsdale, NJ: Lawrence Earlbaum Associates.

Glick, D., Cohen, A., Festinger, E., Xu, D., Li, Q., & Warschauer, M. (2019), Predicting success, preventing faulure. In: Ifenthaler, D., Mah, D., & Yau, J. (eds.). *Utilizing Learning Analytics to Support Study Success.* New York, NY: Springer.

Hooper, S. & Hannafin, M. J. (1988). Cooperative CBI: The effects of heterogeneous versus homogeneous grouping on the learning of progressively complex concepts. *Journal of Educational Computing Research, 4*(4), 413–24.

Houghton Mifflin Harcourt. (2019). Reading inventory. Retrieved from https://www.hmhco.com/programs/reading-inventory.

MetaMetrics. (2019). Lexile framework for reading: Matching readers with text. Retrieved from https://lexile.com/.

Northwest Educational Association. (2019). MAP growth: Precisely measure student growth and performance. Retrieved from https://www.nwea.org/map-growth.

Palacioa, D., et al. (2019). Classroom ability composition and the role of academic performance and school misconduct in the formation of academic and friendship networks. *Journal of School Psychology, 74,* 58–73.

Slavin, R. E. & Karweit, N. (1984). Within-class ability grouping and student achievement. *American Educational Research Association Annual Meeting.* New Orleans.

Thompson, G. W. (1974). The effects of ability grouping upon achievement in eleventh-grade American history. *The Journal on Experimental Education, 42*(4), 76–79.

Part II

TEACHER SUPPORT SYSTEMS

Think back to the building a house analogy. Chapter 1 talked about utilizing a systems perspective when considering school leadership. This systems lens provided the foundation to for the schoolhouse. Chapters 2 through 6 focused specifically on the system of curriculum and instruction, which provides the outer walls, or framing, of the schoolhouse. This system provides the outline and form of a school's purpose—teaching and learning. Chapters 7 through 9 will focus on the Teacher Support Systems that are needed, which provide the vertical support beams of our home. Teachers help support all others in the school; they carry the weight of the work. Therefore, teacher support systems need to be a priority in any and every administrator's mind.

Chapter 7

Professional Development

To keep a lamp burning we have to keep putting oil in it.

—*Mother Theresa*

Quality teacher professional development can be the most underutilized, effective tool at a principal's disposal. Professional development's use to improve teacher skills and enhance certifications has been around for a long time (Baron et al., 2018; Ismat, 1996). In fact, the use of professional development has become more widespread and demanding with new accountability systems. However, teacher complaints about professional development are heard far and wide:

1. The staff development does not pertain to the teacher's field.
2. The staff development was too time consuming, and teachers' plates are already full.
3. The staff development did not show a teacher *how* to do something, just told teachers *to* do something.

Do any of these concerns sound familiar? Teachers enjoy quality professional development that they can utilize and from which they can see the positive effects (Lessing & Witt, 2007); however, teachers are most critical of professional development because they are teachers. Just like doctors can sometimes make the worst patients, teachers can make for difficult students at times. Teachers are critical because they know quality and relevance.

For these reasons, professional development opportunities need to be carefully planned and crafted so that teachers see the value of the opportunities presented. There are many strategies in professional development systems in schools that enable this value to be created and shared. The system must include cycles of professional development, topic determination, delivery methods and times, implementation, as well as evaluation.

CYCLES OF PROFESSIONAL DEVELOPMENT

Think about the professional development opportunities you have enjoyed or employed in the past few years. When was that professional development revisited? How was it reinforced in your building? Did the professional development continue or was it a "One Shot Wonder?" All of these aspects of professional development must be considered, but another pivotal aspect of professional development is often overlooked. This aspect includes the cycles of professional development.

Think for a minute. You are the principal and you have a vision of implementing a quality literacy program with Writing across the Curriculum in your building. You bring in experts to help guide your teachers in the new initiative and spend a few days at the beginning of the year with your teachers and a consultant. Teachers are expected to employ the skills they learned during the school year. You even talk about the initiative in Leadership Team meetings to check on progress. You feel good about the work that is occurring in your building that year. Thus, the school year ends.

A new school year begins, and you hire six new teachers, which is typical turnover with the size of your school. These new teachers begin in August with New Teacher Orientation at the district, and they are anxious to set up their new classrooms. Unfortunately, these teachers do not have much time to get settled and plan instruction before the school year begins. They are nervous about a new job in a new building with new colleagues. Day one of school, and they are off to the races.

What happened to the Writing across the Curriculum initiative? Are there plans to continue that support for teachers who went through the training the year before? What about all of the new teachers who did not have the benefit of the prior year's training? How will they know what to do? To answer these questions, principals must understand that cycles of professional development are essential to create sustained change in schools. Look at figure 7.1 for a representation of what the original cycle should look like.

In providing continued professional development (PD), teachers can get clarification on questions they may have as well as discuss difficulties they may encounter when implementing a new program. This continued PD is needed in order to ensure fidelity of implementation. There are a number of great educational programs out there, but they often do not get the desired results because of fidelity of implementation. Also, continued PD ensures

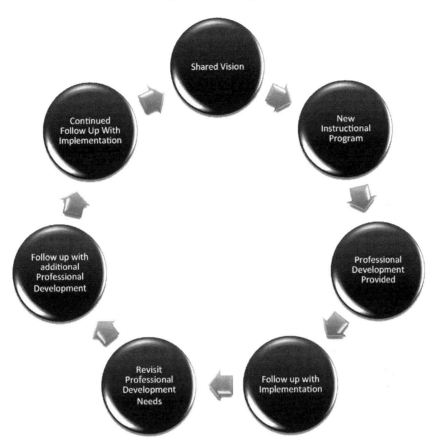

Figure 7.1   Cycle of PD.

that the change continues from one year to the next and conveys a message of priority to the staff.

Administrators often think they cannot continue the PD due to funding restrictions. However, teachers are and should be considered the most valuable resources in a building. Principals, through observations, discussion, and data, should know who is having success in the building with the new program. Tap those individuals to provide continued PD for the rest of the staff, if funding is short. These expert teachers are revered and respected more than an outside consultant in many situations. They are seen as a powerful resource when they find success with a new initiative. They are one of the gang who understands the challenges the rest of the teachers face and, as such, are trusted.

This one cycle of continued PD does not tell the whole story, however. Think, again, about the new teachers joining the faculty. They have not had the benefit of the initial PD experience. Therefore, a principal must create two cycles of PD, one for the tenured faculty and one for the new faculty. These two cycles must run each year in order to help those new teachers stay up to speed on the instructional programs of the school. This necessary cycle is often overlooked and can serve as the most valuable in sustaining a program.

Think about all of the programs implemented in your building. How do new teachers understand the expectations? Is it fair to those teachers to expect them to pick up along with everyone else in the building and stay on track? Sure, other teachers can guide them along the way and share some information, but new teachers are already overwhelmed. Often, new teachers perceive the message, "Hurry up and catch up." This type of induction challenges the fidelity of implementation and often waters down a program.

So, new teachers deserve their own cycle of PD each year. Not only do they participate in the PD provided for all teachers during a school year, but they also should have their own cycle of PD for the initiatives that are deemed a priority in the school but were taught in prior years. The new teacher PD cycle affords new teachers the time and support needed to implement a new program. Lead teachers can and should help support these new teachers in this endeavor, but new teachers deserve and need the initial opportunity to learn and ask questions. See figure 7.2 for the new teacher cycle of PD.

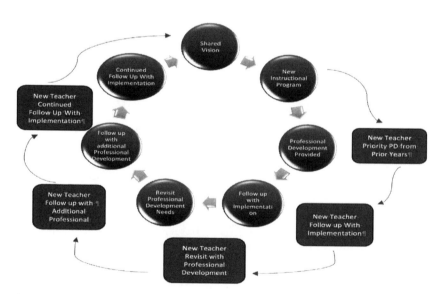

Figure 7.2   New Teacher PD Cycle.

DELIVERY

Time is one of the biggest deterrents to effective teacher PD (Ismat, 1996; Zimmerman & May, 2003). Teachers are already inundated with planning and teaching, additional tasks and challenges associated with the changing role of the teacher, leadership roles in the building, meetings, and the like. When do they have time to seek additional professional learning? The answer is in the valuing of a teacher's time and service; one must embed PD in the teachers' schedules to show the importance of what they are expected to learn.

Embedding the PD shows teachers that their time is valued inside and outside of the school day as well as providing them an avenue for collaboration (Huffman, Hipp, & Pankake, 2001). Embedded PD can take on a few forms and times:

1. During portions of planning periods
2. During early release or late-in scheduled days
3. During Professional Learning Community meetings
4. During predesigned PD days
5. During the regular school day in which teachers are given professional leave to participate

TOPIC DETERMINATION

Who Determines PD?

Teachers need to have a voice in the PD they receive. Teachers will often tell you what they need if only asked. However, often administrators rely on district personnel to dictate PD rather than the teachers themselves. As the vision for the curriculum program is developed in conjunction with the Leadership Team of a school, PD needs to become apparent with the collective capacity of the group (Fullan, 2001b). Also, new state and federal initiatives often direct PD needs, but teachers do not always know what is coming down the pike.

Administrators should know and plan in advance. They should keep teachers informed and ahead of the game so that when new mandates are put in place, teachers are not surprised and are always prepared. This knowledge and preparedness creates a sense of pride and ownership in the achievements of the school. Additionally, staying ahead of the changes to come allows teachers time to work out the kinks prior to a new accountability measure affecting a school's rating. This builds confidence in teachers themselves as well as a confidence in the school leadership.

So, teachers need to know what the district initiatives are, the state and federal mandates that are coming, as well as the school's vision in order to determine PD needs. Additionally, administrators may see needs of which teachers are unaware. As administrators are viewing lesson plans with assessments, needs may become apparent. For example, consider that teachers are turning in their assessments that include rubrics; however, those rubrics are really checklists of a sort. A principal sees this pattern and may consider PD on developing quality rubrics within the school.

Consequently, administrators need to pay attention to what they see while reading lesson plans and during observations. Patterns of behavior may emerge, which can constitute a school-wide PD or a departmental PD that is needed. Additionally, administrators may find there are pockets of teachers who need assistance in certain areas; therefore, PD can target the specific needs of teachers. Of course, conversations need to be held with teachers prior to any PD that is provided. Again, teachers need to understand how and why the PD will help them improve teaching and learning practices within their classrooms in order for value to exist.

When and Why?

Consider that PD cycles should be planned at least two years in advance, but optimally three years in advance. With district and state initiatives as well as school initiatives, teachers can be overwhelmed with change. However, change is a process and does not occur quickly (Fullan, 2002a; Zmuda, Kuklis, & Kline, 2004). Therefore, administrators must plan to implement change in stages so as not to overwhelm teachers and create a revolt. Compare this process to how teachers unwrap an academic standard and plan instruction.

Teachers must go through a process to determine what standards are asking and at what cognitive level, what skills are needed, and what skills students already possess. Without this planning, teachers can miss the mark entirely on instruction, student outcomes, as well as creating frustration for students. If students do not have the necessary skills needed, teachers must plan for that scenario in order to equip students with the necessary skills for success. If students already possess skills, teachers can create boredom among students and never present a challenge for students. The same is true for teachers and PD. See table 7.1 for a comparison of the two processes.

As a result of this process, administrators need to understand the cycles of PD needed as well as the timeline for implementation. Careful design, beginning with the end in mind, allows administrators to work backward and establish a reasonable timeline for skills attainment. This timeline needs to

Table 7.1   Comparing Unwrapping an Academic Standard to Planning PD

Unwrapping an Academic Standard	Planning PD
Identify what the standard is asking of students on a cognitive level.	Identify the intended outcome of the new initiative.
Identify what skills are needed to achieve the desired learning.	Identify what skills are needed to achieve the desired learning.
Identify what subskills are needed to achieve the desired learning.	Identify what subskills are needed to achieve the desired learning.
Plan instruction to assess the preexisting knowledge (pre-assessment).	Determine preexisting knowledge based on observations, lesson planning, and conversations.
Plan instruction with a Backward By Design approach to ensure the building of skill as the unit progresses.	Plan PD with a Backward by Design approach to ensure the building of skills as the initiative progresses.

consider the building of skills over time and the support needed for each skill developed. Additionally, administrators need to know how they will effectively monitor implementation.

Another consideration to answer the question "When?" is to determine when the PD process and cycle will be determined. A strong suggestion is to develop an idea for the PD prior to a Leadership Team meeting. Allow the Leadership Team to review all of the data and initiatives, discuss the skills needed and a reasonable timeline for implementation. If the Leadership Team develops the cycles in collaboration with administration, that same Leadership Team can support the PD plan with the faculty. In this manner, the faculty will not consider the PD thrust upon them, but will understand the "Why?" of it all. This process, assuredly, builds trust among staff.

EVALUATION

All programs within a school should be continuously evaluated to determine their worth in terms of time, resources, and outcomes. This constant evaluation allows for programs to be tweaked and changed in order to best serve the school community. Too often, programs are discontinued for the newest program in education rather than tweaking the existing one and providing additional support, and this practice often results in a waste of time and resources. PD is no different. Once that two to three-year cycle is created, plans to evaluate PD should be included.

How does one evaluate the effectiveness of PD? Just like evaluating a student's academic progress, several data points should be utilized in evaluating the effectiveness of PD:

1. Evidence in Observations
2. Evidence in Lesson Planning
3. Evidence in Student Achievement Results
4. Evidence in teacher conversations
5. Evidence in PD Evaluation Surveys

Let's talk about observations first. If a PD program supports the instructional vision of the school and is carefully thought out with the Leadership Team, then the observation tools used should reflect that initiative in some way. Remember, one must inspect what you expect or the effort can be lost. For example, if a new initiative is part of that instructional vision to improve literacy rates among students at XYZ School, then the literacy initiatives that are being taught and expected to be utilized in the classroom should be part of the observation tool used by the administration.

By designing the observation tool based on initiatives, the administration can collect data on the implementation to include frequency of implementation, fidelity of implementation, student reaction to implementation, and so on. Understandably, the design of the observation tool can either include the initiatives on the tool itself or it can include the direction given to administrators on what to look for and record during observations. Either way, effective data can be collected on the implementation of any new initiative.

Certainly, lesson plans provide another data point to examine when considering a new initiative addressed in PD. Are teachers providing evidence of implementation in lesson plan activities and assessments? How often and to what extent? Administrators need to know to look for those initiatives and collect data from this avenue as well. For example, using the same literacy initiative discussed above, if the lesson plans do not show teachers employing Writing across the Curriculum, which was specifically addressed in PD, then that topic needs to go to the Leadership Team as well as in lesson plan feedback.

What about assessment data? Is there a difference in achievement data that is noticeable since the new implementation? Are common assessment results showing improvement? What about benchmark data? One may not be able to determine results right away on common assessment and benchmarks; however, teachers certainly can see results in a literacy program on the quality of student writing. These results will assuredly be reflected in student grades.

What are teachers saying during the data meetings and planning meetings? These conversations are crucial to understanding how a new program is being implemented in the school. If teachers are not talking about the program when planning, the program is likely not being implemented. Therefore, attending data meetings and at least getting notes from planning meetings is pivotal to the program's success. Discussion should occur about planning instruction with the new program in mind as well as planning assessments.

Teachers will likely discuss what is working along with challenges with any new program, which is crucial for administrators to know and understand in a timely fashion before frustration sets in. Once teachers become frustrated with a new program and do not have the timely support to address the concerns, the likelihood of success diminishes. Therefore, administrators need to be aware and in tune with what the teachers are experiencing and saying about any new program. Likewise, administrators need to be ready to interject and provide additional support at any time.

These support needs to be planned and budgeted in advance. Likely, implementation of a program in our school is not the first of its kind; therefore, principals should anticipate needs and be ready to address them quickly. Administrators should contact other administrators of schools who have experienced success or are implementing a similar change to understand what struggles are being experienced along the way. Building that network of support for principals and teachers can prove invaluable. Remember, you are not reinventing the wheel, and best practice is still best practice.

FREQUENCY

One may wonder how often the PD should be evaluated. Well, informal evaluations occur weekly with observations and lesson plans. The collective data should be shared with the administrative team each week. The same information should be shared with the Leadership Team. Transparency is your friend, and that information will be shared with the staff. Remember, if teachers see you value the new program, so will they. Therefore, informal evaluation occurs daily and weekly.

Along with lesson plans and observations, administrators should check in on teacher conversations about the new initiative. However, these conversations should not be intrusive. Administrators should already be scheduled to participate in planning meetings and data meetings. Do not change the schedule so as to further overwhelm teachers. Just make it a point to discuss the initiative during the regularly scheduled times. Additionally, administrators obviously cannot possibly attend all meetings in large schools; therefore, it is important to know your anchor teachers in the building and ask for their input.

Seeking the advice of teachers on what they think and how a new program is developing in a building is another way to show value for teacher input and decision-making. Teachers appreciate knowing that their opinions matter, and they should. Teachers are the ones engaging in the work of any program, and they have firsthand experience and knowledge about the potential for success or failure of any program in a school. Teachers are the gatekeepers, so to speak. For this reason, seeking their input is just smart.

Additionally, evaluations of the PD should be given to teachers after each PD session. This information is invaluable in planning effective and desired PD for all, and administrators can no longer justify the expense of PD without evaluating its effects (Shaha, Lewis, O'Donnell, & Brown, 2004). Questions should include items that address the content, delivery, and timing.

Teachers should provide input if the PD was helpful, if they feel they can implement with ease, if they need additional support, and so on. Administrators should view these evaluations after each session in order to revise and revamp if necessary. Not only will the PD be better received, but again, teachers will feel value in that their opinions matter. See figure 7.3 for a sample PD evaluation tool.

PD EVALUATION

Date: **Time:**
Name of PD: **Presenter:**

Use the Likert Scale to evaluate the PD you just attended, with the following scale.
1= Strongly Disagree   2= Disagree   3= Neutral   4= Agree   5= Strongly Agree

1.   The PD presented is useful to me personally.

       1   2   3   4   5

2.   The PD presented is useful to my team.

       1   2   3   4   5

3. The format of the PD was conducive to learning.

       1   2   3   4   5

4. The presenter appeared knowledgeable.

       1   2   3   4   5

5. I found the PD effective.

       1   2   3   4   5

6. What questions do you still have?

7. How can I further assist you?

Figure 7.3   Sample PD Evaluation.

PULSE CHECKS

In addition to all of the evaluation discussed earlier, it is important to administer surveys a few times a year to gauge implementation and understanding. These surveys should not be long and can be given in paper format or electronically. The data from these surveys should be used in the Leadership Team meetings when discussing the following year's PD cycles as well as to determine the need to slow down or speed up the implementation during the current year.

Understandably, administration should expect an implementation dip with any change (Fullan, 2001a), and address the cause of the dip: either a fear of change itself or the lack of skills needed to implement the change (Dewitt, 2017; Fullan, 2007). Just like in classroom instruction, the need to monitor and adjust exists with PD if one expects to achieve the desired results: change and student growth.

Furthermore, teachers may fill out a PD evaluation immediately after the PD but feel differently about it once they have had time to work with the initiative a little. This change can determine the need for more resources and support or the need to accelerate the timeline in the PD cycles. Therefore, pulse checks are important to administer and understand from an administrative perspective. Ideally, pulse checks should be given three to four times a year, including the end of the year. Again, teachers will tell you what they need if only asked. See figure 7.4 for a sample pulse check.

END-OF-YEAR PLANNING

Collectively, the data from observations, conversations, lesson plans, student achievement results, PD surveys, and pulse checks should be compiled. This data paints a pretty clear picture of an instructional program in a school. Removing one element from this compilation may mislead an administrative team as to where to allocate resources and plan PD for the following year. Of course, knowing district and state initiatives, as discussed before, should also be a part of this planning.

Based on the planning, administrators and teachers should realize that the two- to three-year plan is organic. Changes occur and should be expected each year. However, the direction of any PD initiative should remain clear for all stakeholders. The results of all data points should be shared with the stakeholders so that they understand where they are in the process of implementation, what strengths have been exhibited and celebrated, as well as what challenges are yet to come.

Pulse Check Survey

1. Based on your data, what professional development would be beneficial to your team?

2. What professional development would benefit you personally?

3. Based on school data, what professional development needs do you think exist?

Sample Pulse Check Survey

Figure 7.4   Sample Pulse Check Survey.

Understanding the "Why?" behind PD goes a long way in teacher morale and support. Without teacher ownership in any program, the program will be less successful, as working together provides the needed support for change and collective accountability (Bresicha et al., 2019; Guskey, 1994; Zmuda, Kuklis & Kline, 2004).

Therefore, administrators should be intimately knowledgeable about each step in the process, the stages of the process, the success and struggles of teachers, as well as the success and struggles of students in order to plan effectively for the following year. In doing so, administrators also show ownership and value in providing quality teacher support through quality PD.

SYSTEMS APPROACH

In order to develop a system's approach to PD, principals must consider all of the cycles of PD needed. After viewing all of the data with the Leadership

Team, administrators need to classify the PD needed and strategically plan the particulars and importance of each proposal. See figure 7.5 for a representation of all four cycles that must be considered and planned.

In reviewing the four cycles of PD, principals must acknowledge that Professional Learning Communities (PLC's) can provide valuable professional development for teachers if the meetings are run correctly. In these meetings, teachers should focus on planning instruction and assessments, analyzing departmental data, discussing best teaching practices, and examining student quality of work. Each meeting should have a focus and a protocol to follow so that teachers remain on track. See figure 7.6 for a sample PLC protocol.

The topics of all teacher PD and new teacher PD were addressed earlier. However, what about focused PD? Imagine that the math department needs help with teaching conceptual understanding versus linear problem solving—this is a focus for a specific department. The entire school does not need to participate in this PD, just the math teachers. The same can be said for English teachers trying to teach metacognition in reading. Only English teachers

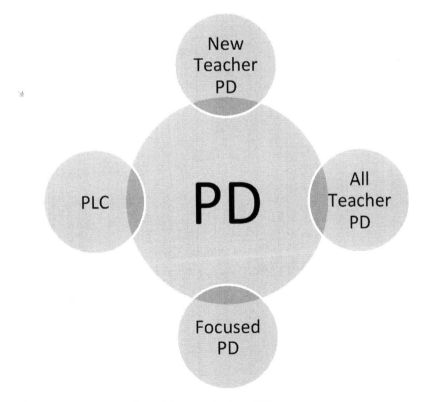

Figure 7.5   Representation of the Four Cycles of PD.

PLC
Lesson Planning/Assessment Building

PLC Team: **Meeting Date:**   **Meeting Time:**

Members Present:	Members Absent:

Team Norms: (Must be agreed upon)

School Goal: (From SRP)	
Team Goal: (Based on data)	
Focus questions: (Lesson Plans? Assessments? Data?)	
Discussion and Plans:	
Unanswered Questions:	Next meeting: Agenda items:

- Attach Agenda

Figure 7.6   Sample PLC Protocol.

need this assistance. Of course, the examination of student work in relation to the cognitive level of the standards can help guide this work.

SUMMARY

Teacher PD is a valuable tool for administrators and teachers alike. PD should be based on the instructional vision of the school as well as the district, state, and federal initiatives that may be coming down the pike. Staying ahead of the changes to come allows the change to become a process rather than an event. Teachers should be asked what they need in terms of PD as well.

The Leadership Team along with the principal should develop the PD cycles two to three years in advance, knowing that the plan is organic. Two cycles of PD should exist: one for tenured teachers and one for new teachers. Data should be collected from lesson plans, observations, conversations, and achievement data in order to determine effectiveness of PD. Additionally, teachers should evaluate PD right after it is given to help plan for the most effective PD throughout a year.

Lastly, pulse check surveys should be given to teachers throughout the year to determine stages of implementation and additional supports needed. All of the data collected should be shared in the end-of-the-year planning with the Leadership Team to determine the PD cycles for the following years.

PD content, cycles, and planning should never happen without the input of those to be affected. Teachers need a clear voice in aspects of PD if true learning is intended to take place. Isn't that the point, after all?

A PIECE AT A TIME

- How many cycles of PD should an administrator plan for? Explain.
- What are teachers' chief complaints about PD?
- How should PD topics be determined? By Whom? Why?
- When should PD be provided for teachers?
- What are the five methods to evaluate PD?
- Why should pulse checks be administered throughout the year?
- Who should be part of the end-of-year planning and why?

REFERENCES

Baron, C., Sklarwitz, S., Bang, H. & Shatara, H. (2018). Understanding what teachers gain from professional development in historic sites. *Theory & Research in Social Education, 47*(1), 76–107.

Brezicha, K., Ikoma, S., Park, H. & LeTendre, G. (2019). The ownership perception gap: exploring teacher job satisfaction and its relationship to teachers' and princpals' perception of decision-making opportunities. *International Journal of Leadership in Education,* 1–29. DOI: 10.1080/13603124.2018.1562098

Dewitt, P. (2017). *Collaborative leadership: Six influences that matter most.* Thousand Oaks, CA: Corwin.

Fullan, M. (2001a). *The new meaning of educational change* (3rd ed.). New York: Teachers College Press.

Fullan, M. (2001b). *Leading in a culture of change.* San Francisco, CA: Jossey Bass.

Fullan, M. (2002). The change leader. *Educational Leadership, 59*(8), 16–21.

Fullan, M. (2007). *The new meaning of educational change* (4th ed.). New York, NY: Teachers College Press.

Guskey, T. R. (1994). Professional development in education: The search for the optimal mix. Proceedings from the AERA 1994: *The Annual Meeting of the American Educational Research Association.* New Orleans, LA.

Huffman, J. B., Hipp, K. A., Pankake, A. M., & Moller, G. (2001). Professional learning communities: Leadership, purposeful decision making, and job-embedded staff development. *Journal of School Leadership, 11*(5), 448–63.

Ismat, A. (1996). Making time for teacher professional development. Retrieved form ERIC database (ED 400259).

Lessing, A., & De Witt, M. (2017). The value of continuous professional development: Teachers' perceptions. *South African Journal of Education, 27*(1), 53–67.

Shaha, S., Lewis, V., O'Donnell, T., & Brown, D. (2004). Evaluating professional development: An approach to verifying impact on teachers and students. *The Journal of Research in Professional Learning,* National Staff Development Council.

Zimmerman, J., & May, J. (2003). Providing effective professional development: What's holding us back? *American Secondary Education, 31*(2), 37–48.

Zmuda, A., Kuklis, R., & Kline, E. (2004). *Transforming schools: Creating a culture of continuous improvement.* Alexandria, VA: ASCD.

Chapter 8

New Teacher Supports

The mediocre teacher tells. The good teacher explains. The superior teacher demonstrates. The great teacher inspires.

—*William Arthur Ward*

Every administrator knows that new teachers need the most support. Imagine they have just graduated from school and often feel they are ready to change the world. However, these same teachers quickly become overwhelmed and exhausted. In fact, this inevitable feeling of being overwhelmed does not take long to rear its ugly head. New teachers are bombarded with so many new challenges.

Not only do these new teachers have to learn the culture of their new school, the processes and procedures in the new school, the district policies, and who to go to for specific needs, but they also have to learn how to effectively plan, collaborate, teach, and assess the district curriculum. In this large list, there is no mention of technology systems that must be mastered, like grading, attendance, discipline, technology integration in teaching, and the like.

First-year teachers work the hardest because everything is so new and needs to be understood and learned all at once. There is no time for a change *process* in this instance; first-year teachers have a steep and fast learning curve. So, how do administrators support new teachers? A discussion about new teacher PD can be found in the prior chapter. This cycle of PD is the most overlooked and the most needed in many instances. Providing new teachers their own cycle of PD is the only way to ensure that the school truly has a *shared* instructional vision.

However, a myriad of ways to provide additional new teacher support come to mind, and efforts spent with new teachers will never be wasted. Working with new teachers creates a better morale on the most taxed, loyalty in the face of teacher shortages, and the best learning environment for students (Moir & Gless, 2001). However, it should all begin prior to the teacher being hired.

VISION

Interview Process

When a teacher interviews for a job, the tone of the interview sets the stage for the expectations and support to follow and can serve as a recruitment tool itself (Barber, Hollenbeck, Tower, & Phillips, 1994). Think about it for a minute. Questions regarding teaching and learning surely are included in the interview process. These questions inform the new teacher about instructional priorities in the school as well as establish the principal's role in those priorities. Consider the following questions in table 8.1 and what the questions reveal during an interview process.

With each answer, the principal can expound upon the school's program and the supports that exist to assist teachers in their efforts while sharing the vision of the school. Now consider when it is time for the teacher candidate to ask questions. During this period, the principal weaves in the conversation the teacher support systems in the school, school culture, and expressed enthusiasm for the instructional program at the school. New teachers will understand the focus of the school and the support systems that exist, enabling that teacher to make an informed decision about a potential job based on a shared vision.

Table 8.1   Interview Questions and Their Subsequent Reveal

Interview Question	Question Reveal
Describe how you plan a unit from beginning to end.	Focus on planning instruction—Vision
How and when do you respond when students are not learning. How do you know?	Focus on formative and summative assessment, remediation, and differentiated instruction—Vision
How do you challenge and enrich the more advanced learner?	Focus on differentiation—Vision
What do you expect from your administrator?	Focus on leadership's role of support in the school—Vision

Orientation

School-Based Orientation

Most schools offer a new teacher orientation of sorts. This orientation is generally a treasure hunt to tour the building and learn who performs what roles in the building, where to find needed supplies and equipment, and how to access district resources. However, despite the importance of each of these items on an agenda, the important information is missing—the expectations for the instructional program of the school.

In order to best support new teachers, it is best to provide a couple of days of orientation to the instructional program of the school—planning with colleagues to include long-range planning and unit planning, daily lesson planning, and creating assessments. This type of instructional orientation will not only allow new teachers to build rapport with their colleagues prior to school beginning, but will also provide a sense of calm regarding the tasks that are before them. The beginning of the year is hectic for all teachers, but especially for new teachers.

Long-range plans are typically due within a month of school starting; however, teachers should have the long-range plan mapped out prior to beginning instruction. It only makes sense that, as a traveler, you would have read the road map before you would begin the trip, right? The instructional orientation provides time and support to complete these long-range plans, which also supports beginning instruction. Teachers who are prepared for the first week of instruction set the tone for their students, and students can smell teacher's confidence or lack thereof.

Including lesson planning and unit instruction in the instructional orientation also strongly supports the teacher in that teachers then know what planning expectations are, what technology is used for plan submission—all which give teachers another level of comfort and confidence. In contrast, leaving new teachers to figure the process out on their own creates anxiety and sometimes fear they are not meeting expectations. Understanding assessments and assessment policies in the school will also help build teacher self-efficacy, which directly impacts student achievement (Goe & Stickler, 2008).

District-based Orientation

School districts often provide a new teacher orientation as well; however, this orientation typically focuses on benefits, district technology, district policies, teacher evaluation, and the like. Again, all of the areas are important for new teachers, and certainly these teachers leave a district new teacher orientation dazed and inundated with thoughts of the tasks to come. As new teachers embark on beginning their careers, they are more focused on more logistical priorities first.

New teachers are often concerned about moving to the area of their new schools, finding and setting up their classrooms, finding out what they will be teaching, and securing any textbook materials that may assist. Most certainly, these tasks are important and fulfill the lower rungs of Maslow's Hierarchy of Needs. Teachers often think about students and if their needs are being met, but do administrators think about teachers within this same framework? If not, they should.

Maslow's Hierarchy of Needs was developed by Maslow Herzberg in the 1950s to describe the personal needs people experience in their workplace. Maslow constructed a linear progression of needs, postulating that one could not fulfill a need until the prior need in the hierarchy was fulfilled (Gawel, 1997). As such, this theory has been used in business and education arenas. However, education has primarily referenced this theory when dealing with students' needs, not the teachers' needs themselves.

In order for teachers to become self-actualized with a strong sense of self-efficacy, they must first have their physiological and safety needs met. Landing that first job with benefits and finding a place to live that provides shelter and safety are the first priorities for any new education graduate. However, what do administrators do to help new teachers feel a sense of belonging and friendship? The instructional new teacher orientation provides time for new teachers to build rapport with their colleagues and a sense of belonging within their respective departments and other new teachers.

As opposed to the treasure hunt model of new teacher orientation, in an instructional orientation, teachers are forced to engage. Not only are administrators assisting with the belonging needs on Maslow's chart, but they are also assisting with the esteem needs, which provide a sense of confidence, respect, and achievement (Maslow, 1970). Only when physiological, safety, belonging, and esteem needs are met can an individual move to problem solving and creativity. See Maslow's Hierarchy of Needs in figure 8.1.

Therefore, new teacher orientations and district orientations are pivotal in meeting the needs of beginning teachers. Without quality orientations, teachers will not be able to climb the hierarchy of needs and become the efficient and effective teachers they desire in their first year in the profession.

MENTORS

Expectations

Every new teacher to a building needs a mentor, whether that individual is a new teacher to the profession or not. Mentors for tenured teachers new to the building are intended to fulfill some of those same hierarchical needs

Figure 8.1 Maslow's Hierarchy of Needs (Maslow, 1970).

discussed above as well as serve as a resource for school policies, processes, and procedures. However, new teachers to the profession need a more in-depth mentor, like a big brother or sister. New teachers to the profession need someone they can trust explicitly to provide constructive feedback, to share ideas, to lend a shoulder to cry on, as well as provide support for school policies, processes, and procedures.

When considering a new teacher mentor program, many elements must be prioritized and defined.

1. Does the mentor teach the same content or subject? This is not required but preferable.
2. Does the mentor share the same planning period? This is necessary to provide easier access to open lines of communication.
3. Will the personalities of the mentor and mentee mesh? This may seem inconsequential, but this factor certainly is not. Without complimentary personalities, the mentor could be misunderstood as well as the mentee, creating conflict or mistrust (Kottke & Kimura, 2009).
4. Are the mentor program expectations clear to both the mentor and the mentee? The expectations of the program should be in writing and agreed upon by both parties.

Mentors play a very valuable role in shaping school culture (Ingersoll, 2001; Johnson & Johnson, 2002), and this is why it is important that administrators build the mentor pool within their schools. Some states require that an official mentor must be certified to be considered a mentor, and this certification requires some training on the state's evaluation system. This additional training is useful in that part of the mentor's responsibility should be to guide the new teacher through the first year of evaluation. Therefore, administrators need to be willing to send teachers to training so that the best qualified teachers serve as mentors.

Clearly defining the expectations of the mentorship, as stated above, is pivotal prior to starting the newly forged relationship. Both parties need to understand the parameters of the relationship and the goal. Areas to include in the mentor curriculum should include more than just teacher evaluation. What about instructional planning and assessment? Mentees should be guided through the process on more than one occasion. However, mentees must feel respected as professionals and not diminished just because they are new.

Additionally, school culture, processes, and procedures should be shared at multiple intervals as well as advice with instructional strategies and classroom discipline. Both of the latter factors will affect the learning culture of the classroom. Most first-year teachers are most nervous about classroom discipline (Browers & Tomic, 2000; Veenman, 1984), as these new, young, professionals are now responsible for the behavior of many young people in addition to their own behaviors. For some, leaving the nest and becoming responsible for more than just yourself can be daunting.

However, these same teachers most likely do not connect the dots between instructional strategies and engagement with student discipline. They can become focused on the behavior itself and not the preexisting conditions that make the behavior possible. Where there are strong, engaging and differentiated instructional strategies, classroom discipline is minimized (McCleod, Fisher, & Hoover, 2003).

This mentor relationship should last the entire school year. Mentees and mentors should have agreed-upon scheduled times to meet to ensure the proper support is provided. After all, teachers, like everyone else, get very busy, and remembering to check in and provide specific support may not be prioritized or even remembered because of a typical, hectic school day. The new teacher mentee, often besieged, will not remember on her own to ask the necessary questions. However, those same new teachers will certainly reflect on any mentor program as to whether or not the program was helpful. Therefore, scheduled times are necessary.

Principal's Role

Other types of mentorships exist within the school as well. For example, what about the relationship between the principal and the new teacher? The principal needs to have a true open-door policy for these new teachers when it comes to school matters as well as being available to assist in areas outside of teaching. It is not outlandish to think a principal would help new teachers find housing in the area or help new teachers find doctors they can trust. Principals can be seen as a school parent. Ever heard of a work spouse? Why not a work parent?

Developing this type of principal-to-teacher mentorship with new teachers truly makes the new teachers trust the principal and see the principal as a resource. Furthermore, new teachers will feel a sense of loyalty to principals who assist teachers professionally and personally. Certainly, loyalty to a principal is one of the key indicators of a teacher's tenure at a school, and continuity in good teaching staff builds a foundation for excellence. Additionally, this relationship creates a culture of family, and this culture benefits every stakeholder involved. More discussion on culture will follow in volume 2 of this book.

Principals should also provide frequent feedback to new teachers. Classroom observations should be frequent for new teachers for a couple of reasons:

1. The goal is to develop, shape, and mold new teachers. All teachers need to see that the principal is invested in developing and supporting the teaching faculty of a school. Remember, where teachers see principals spend their time is what teachers see principals value. This point cannot be stressed enough.
2. Frequent observations provide an avenue for frequent conversations and great feedback. The value of feedback is immeasurable, depending on how it is presented. If presented in the manner it is intended, to provide praise and development, then the new teacher further develops trust in the principal.
3. Without conversations and frequent observations, how will a principal know the strengths and weaknesses of a teacher, if additional support is needed, and if the teacher warrants a contract renewal?

New teacher meetings with the principal several times a year, maybe once a quarter, are also warranted. These meetings allow for new teachers to continue their collaboration and collegiality as well as provide valuable feedback to principals. Just like teachers need feedback on their performance, principals need the same (Campo, 1993). Not only does the new teacher group provide a fresh perspective for the principal, but this group shows the new teachers that the principal is vested in their success.

Principals should seek feedback on the mentor program, what is working in the school, what is not working in the school, as well as how the administration could further serve the teachers. Remembering that the leadership style is bottom up rather than top down is important. An administrator's job should be to support teachers, not dictate to them. This feedback should come from not only the mentees but the mentors as well. Established teachers have valuable input on the programs as well.

Considering the importance of the principal's role in the development and support of teachers, why is it that so many principals do not engage at the level needed? Time constraints is the number one answer among administrators. The constant barrage of demands and the need to put out fires serves as a hindrance to many. Consequently, if a principal spends all of his/her time on student discipline and *not* serving as the instructional leader of the school, then teachers will not value the instructional vision of the school either.

Rewards

Mentors who are certified to serve in that capacity often receive recertification points from their districts and states for their efforts. Because of the time commitment, mentors should be rewarded in some way, and not only through recertification points. What if a mentor does not need recertification points? If that is the only reward, beside the intrinsic one to help a colleague, what is the motivation?

Mentors in a school should be considered as school leaders (Moir & Bloom, 2003). Teachers, just like any other employee, want to feel valued in the workplace. The personal request by a principal to be a mentor to a new teacher demonstrates a principal's confidence and esteem for a teacher and the teacher's craft. Additionally, these mentor teachers should be recognized among their peers, which provides motivation for others to follow suit. Special distinctions for mentors can include school garb, recognition at new teacher meetings, recognition at faculty meetings, recognition in school publications to include social media and print publications, and so on. The more recognition the more prestigious the role.

Of course, teachers will never turn down additional pay, as they are traditionally underpaid. Providing a stipend to teacher mentors does not have to be exorbitant; however, a stipend does show teachers that you understand the value of their time. If the budget does not allow for a commiserate stipend to match the time expended, then a simple explanation and an expressed desire to do more goes a long way. Teacher pay is not the number one reason teachers leave a school. Teachers leave a principal, not a school (Fredricks, 2001). Never undervalue the value of expressed appreciation.

EVALUATION

How do you evaluate the effectiveness of new teacher supports? Evaluating school programs is necessary and often unused tool for school improvement.

To evaluate new teacher supports, administrators can look in a few places: the new teachers themselves via conversations and surveys, rates of recidivism, successful teacher evaluations and teacher morale.

Just like with students, if you ask new teachers what is working or what is not, they will tell you. These questions should be asked in the new teacher meetings as well as via surveys. Surveys, as mentioned earlier, should be given a few times a year and should not take up too much of the teacher's time because teachers are busy and often get inundated with surveys. Long surveys may require more time than the teacher has to give at that moment. By the time the teacher finds time, the survey may be forgotten.

Consequently, the information that you can glean from an anonymous survey is valuable, in that the respondent does not feel pressure to answer in a certain way due to fear of repercussion. Also, the mentor should ask the new teacher periodically what he/she can do better to orient and assist the new teacher. The findings should be reported back to administration in order to best develop a successful new teacher support program. All feedback is needed and welcome. Remember, the more time vested in new teachers, the more likely they are to stay.

Teacher turnover rates tell a tale. Teachers change schools due to long travel times from home to work, for sure. However, a teacher will travel further for a school with a supportive climate. Teachers talk. News of a school in which the teacher feels valued and supported travels fast, but the news of a school with a toxic culture travels faster. Therefore, if teachers are happy, they are less likely to look for greener pastures. With the current rates and national issues with teacher shortages, administrators want good teachers to return each year.

Teacher evaluations and teacher morale are also good gauges of successful new teacher support systems. If teachers feel prepared and confident in their second year of teaching, then the mentors and administrators did a good job of preparing them. Evaluation systems vary by state; however, evaluation by its very connation can be stressful. Therefore, the most prepared are less anxious. With a climate of support, teacher morale is higher. Teachers need to feel safe to make mistakes (Phelps, 2010) and remain supported nonetheless. Teacher morale in a building can be tangible, felt as soon as one enters the doors. If the new teachers are supported and remain enthusiastic, they are more likely to stay in the profession.

Teacher morale is assessed each year in most states via a state survey. This survey is used on many school evaluations or school report cards. However, the pulse check surveys discussed in a prior chapter are also good gauges to progress monitor morale and teacher supports so that an end-of-the-year survey does not yield surprising results. No one likes an ugly autopsy report. It is always best practice to progress monitor along the way to monitor and adjust if necessary.

A SYSTEMS APPROACH

Simply put, administrators must plan for successful new teacher supports. These supports must include more than mentor teachers and traditional orientations. See figure 8.2 for all of the elements of new teacher supports.

Of course, each component must be planned and evaluated for its effectiveness in order to create an effective, supportive environment. Not included in the graphic is the principal's role in nurturing new teachers. This may include helping a teacher find a doctor or a roommate. Administrators find themselves taking on additional roles to create a family atmosphere among staff. With the national teacher shortage, each piece and part is vital for the future of the profession.

SUMMARY

New teachers need the most support as they begin their careers, as they can quickly become inundated. Addressing the needs of new teachers can be compared to Maslow's Hierarchy of Needs. New teachers must progress through the hierarchy in order to develop problem solving and creativity in their classrooms. These supports and hierarchical progressions begin in the

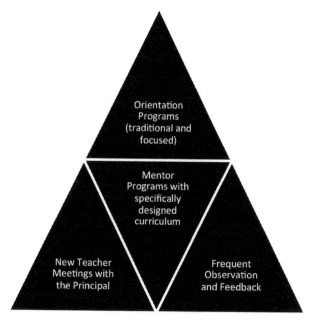

Figure 8.2   Elements of New Teacher Support Programs.

interview, where administrators communicate their visions for the school and how teachers are supported within the school.

New teacher orientations at both the district and school level need to be carefully thought out and planned, and school orientations need to include more than just a "Who's Who." Instructional orientations with departmental colleagues provide an avenue to truly help teachers feel prepared for the first week of school, with addressing areas such as long-range planning, unit planning, building assessments, and so on.

A New Teacher Mentor program should be established that is well-defined and timely. Mentors should be selected carefully, and personalities, planning periods, subjects taught, and timing should be considered. These mentors should be revered as leaders in the school and should be rewarded for their efforts. Expressing value for teacher mentor time and talent will serve to motivate others to follow suit. Principals also play a pivotal role in new teacher mentoring by providing professional and personal support.

Evaluating the effectiveness of a new teacher support program is important so that administrators can monitor and adjust, if needed. This evaluation can and should occur multiple times a year through varied avenues: surveys, conversations, teacher evaluations, and rates of recidivism. Teacher shortages across the nation dictate that principals take a lead role in ensuring teachers feel supported and successful.

A PIECE AT A TIME

- How is the school's vision and understanding of teacher supports in a school first communicated to new teachers?
- Describe three different types of new teacher orientation?
- How can Maslow's Hierarchy of Needs be met for new teachers? Describe each level.
- What elements should be included in a successful new teacher mentor program?
- How can mentors be rewarded for their time and efforts?
- What is the principal's role in new teacher supports?
- Name at least three ways to determine if a new teacher support system is successful.

REFERENCES

Barber, A., Hollenbeck, J., Tower, S., & Phillips, J. (1994). The effects of interview focus and recruitment effectiveness: A field experiment. *Journal of Applied Psychology, 79*(6), 886–96.

Browers, A. & Tomic, W. (2000). A longitudinal study of teacher burnout and perceived self-efficacy in classroom management. *Teaching and Teacher Education, 16*(2), 239–53.

Campo, C. (1993). Collaborative school cultures: How principals make a difference. *School Organization, 13*(2), 119–37.

Fredricks, J. (2001). Why teachers leave. *Education Digest, 66*(8), 46–48.

Gawel, J. (1997). Herzberg's theory of motivation and Maslow's hierarchy of needs. *Practical Assessment, Research & Evaluation, 5*(11). http://PAREonline.net/getvn.asp?v=5&n=11.

Goe, L. & Stickler, L. (2008). *Teacher quality and student achievement: Making the most of recent research.* Washington, DC: National Comprehension Center for Teacher Quality.

Ingersoll, R. (2001). Teacher turnover and teacher shortages: An organizational analysis. *American Education Research Journal, 38*(3), 499–534.

Johnson, S. & Kardos, S. (2002). Keeping new teachers in mind. *Educational Leadership, 59*(6), 12–16.

Kottke, J. & Kamuri, S. (2009). Assessing individuals for team "worthiness": Investigating the intersection of the big five personality factors, organizational citizenship behavior, and teamwork aptitude. In: Lauren Palcroft & Melissa Lopez (eds.), *Personality Assessment: New Research* (pp. 63–93). NY: Nova Science Publishers, Inc.

Maslow, A. H. (1970). *Motivation and personality* (2nd ed.). New York: Harper and Row.

McLeod, J., Fisher, J., & Hoover, G. (2003). *The key elements of classroom management: Managing time and space, student behavior and instructional strategies.* Alexandria, VA: ASCD.

Moir, E. & Bloom, G. (2003). Fostering leadership through mentoring. *Educational Leadership, 60*(8), 58–60.

Moir, E. & Gless, G. (2001). Quality induction: An investment in teachers. *Teacher Education Quarterly, 28*(1), 109–114.

Phelps, P. (2010). Helping teachers become leaders. *The Clearing House: A Journal of Educational Strategies, Issues and Ideas, 81*(3), 119–22.

Veenman, S. (1984). Perceived problems of beginning teachers. *Review of Educational Research, 54*(2), 143–78.

Chapter 9

Teacher Leadership

If your actions inspire others to dream more, learn more, do more and become more, you are a leader.

—*President John Quincey Adams*

SPECIFIC ASSET

One of the first things an administrator needs to understand about teachers is that their content knowledge is their specific asset, or their construed expertise and value. This expertise needs to be respected and consulted often in order for teachers to feel valued. Let's face it. A principal cannot be an expert in all areas and often do not have all of the answers when dealing with students. It simply is not possible. However, when teachers are consulted and valued for their expertise and knowledge, they often emerge as leaders in the building. Recognizing and rewarding this type of teacher leadership is a large part of a teacher support system.

Think about an accounting ledger for a moment. In the left-hand column are the input factors and on the right-hand column are the output factors. For a teacher, the left column includes their experiences, training and knowledge—the assets they bring to the table. In the right-hand column, the output is student learning and school culture. The input directly affects the output. The ledger, in order to be balanced, has to include teacher knowledge and experience.

Does that mean that teachers have the last word on all curricular and student issues? No, it does not. However, teachers need to understand how and why decisions are made. Being part of the process helps them to understand the "why" surrounding a decision, which has a greater impact on acceptance and ownership.

How does including teachers in the decision-making process show teacher support? Simply put, teachers often feel that changes and decisions are made for them, not with them. In doing so, programs and ideas are thrust upon them without valuing their assets. A close parallel is when a child asks a parent why the parent has made a specific decision, or the child is challenging the parent's decision-making. When a parent responds, "Because I said so!" the child is often angry and feels diminished in that his voice was not heard.

This is not to say that a parent doesn't have veto power over their children, because they do. However, the same rationale applies. Teachers do not want to be treated in such a matter; they are adults with skills and they wanted to be treated as such.

KNOWLEDGE BASE ASSUMPTIONS
AND CHALLENGES

One of the most valuable assumptions a principal can grasp and fully embrace is that the job of the principalship is bigger than any one person. One person cannot do it alone, at least not effectively. Just as the teachers' specific asset is their knowledge and skills; principals need to understand that their most valuable asset is their staff. A staff of highly qualified and motivated professionals will make a school successful, despite the principal.

Consequently, a staff of unmotivated, unsupported, and disconnected staff will surely make a school fail. Therefore, principals need to value their staffs by not only supporting them but also sharing the successes of the school. After all, teachers are the ones doing the work in the trenches.

Valuing teachers' assets and including them in the decision-making process affords teachers the opportunity to feel that have a voice, even if the voice doesn't change the outcome. Social theory has long dictated that social approval is desired by all (Lindenberg, 1990; Maslow, 1970). Therefore, each teacher's ideas and concerns should be considered in order for teachers to feel that approval. Only when teachers receive that social approval will they then give the same social approval to the administration which often has to make unpopular decisions (Lindenberg, 1996).

All of this is to say that administrators must understand that in order to effectively lead, teachers have to want to follow. Otherwise, administrators have a lonely walk ahead of them, and schools are less effective. Therefore, it is important for administrators to understand the needs of their entire staff, faculty and staff included.

In doing so, administrators have to be willing to adjust their leadership styles to meet the needs of the people they are trying to lead. Each individual has his or her own leadership style, but the needs of the masses vary; your leadership style might not match the needs of others. Therefore, administrators need to take stock of the needs of their faculties and adjust accordingly.

No one can argue that the field of education is comprised mostly of women. Understanding the makeup and gender roles and expectations in a school only serves to understand the needs of faculty. In fact, Ridgeway (1997) concluded that a workplace can have a gender identity, and this factor plays a role on social norms within the institution. Social norms between men and women are often found to be different.

Additionally, faculty members hold perceived leadership expectations of principals based on their gender: there are shared beliefs about individuals based on their gender roles (Eagly, Wood, & Diekman, 2000). Basically, men are expected to behave in one manner and women are typically expected to behave in another. So, what happens when a leader does not conform to societal norms and expectations?

When expectation does not match reality, challenges ensue. The truth is that different types of leadership styles are needed in different scenarios. Typically, women are stronger in the collaborative and transformational leadership arenas, and men are stronger in the transactional leadership and laissez faire leadership arenas (Eagly & Johannesen-Schmidt, 2001). However, all types of leadership styles are needed in the same institution to meet the needs of all at different times. Schools are not cookie-cutter in that it is comprised of complex human beings who are not all the same.

Recognizing the needs of individuals and understanding preconceived notions based on gender is pivotal to effective leadership and is a challenge for many. Think about the scenario with an experienced teacher who is phenomenal in the classroom but has been timid about leadership. This teacher may need a collaborative approach when put in a leadership position but a more laissez faire approach when in the classroom. Differentiation is needed when applying leadership approaches, just like differentiation is needed in the classroom.

Leaders must understand the differences between men and women and their needs in order to provide the best support. Just as students, teachers need to be set up for success, not failure. Teacher leaders need to understand the same about those peers they wish to lead as well. Teacher leaders may have a more difficult time in differentiation their leadership styles because they are perceived as an equivalent peer, which provides more challenges as well.

AVENUES

Within a school, there are a plethora of opportunities for teachers to lead. The opportunities need to be clear and widely known within the school for individuals to accept the roles, both from the leadership perspective and the perspective of the led. Meaning, transparency is key in order for the systems to work. There can be no hidden agendas or informal leadership structures. Lack of transparency is the quickest way to create doubt and mistrust; whereas, transparency and positivity have a direct impact on the level of trust placed in a principal and the perceived effectiveness of leadership (Norman, Avolio, & Luthans, 2010).

Traditional Teacher Leadership

Traditional avenues for teacher to lead include a school's Leadership Team, a school improvement council, and departmental leadership. These fundamental roles should be considered as part of the entire Leadership Team of the school. Individuals who assume these roles should be respected and accepted by their peers. As such, these individuals have a representative voice of the entire faculty; consequently, this voice does not always and should not always be one of assent. Principals need those who will strive to understand and sometimes challenge decisions. Varying opinions lead to the most effective practices and best support.

When different opinions are shared and all contributions are respected and valued, a thorough discussion can follow. Let's face it: the collective intelligence of a staff far outweighs that of an individual. The principal may know limitations, policy, and funding issues that the staff does not, and this information should be shared. Principals must share their understandings and beliefs with the faculty, and this relational transparency will help build trust and a positive affective culture in the school (Kernis, 2003). In doing so, the best decision can be made for a school that all parties can accept and live by. In this instance, acceptance leads to ownership.

A good analogy is that of a stool. Consider one leg of the stool as the school district's direction that works in conjunction with the state's direction, with the second leg of the stool representing the principal's understanding of how to achieve that direction. The third leg is the opinion of the teacher leadership in how to achieve that direction. All three legs are intended to achieve a vision. However, if teacher leadership is not represented, the stool is not balanced and will not hold the weight of the work to be done. See figure 9.1 for the balance of leadership needed in a school.

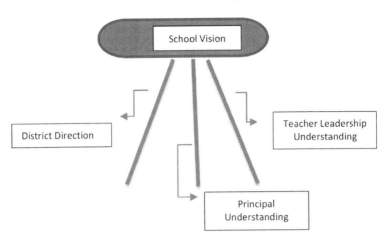

Figure 9.1   The Balance of Leadership.

Student Organizations

Teachers also have opportunities to lead with student organizations within a school, such as faculty sponsors of groups like student government, robotics, band/choral directors, athletic coaches, and content area groups like the French Club. All of these avenues of leadership are important to the teachers as well as the students. However, how do administrators show they value these avenues of teacher leadership as much as the traditional roles? Principals must demonstrate their appreciation and support for each and every type of leadership role assumed by teachers. This appreciation can come in the form of recognition, stipends, and presence.

Principals cannot underestimate the power of their presence. Visibility has been shown consistently to correlate to best practices in instructional leadership, which directly impacts student engagement (Quinn, 2002; Whitaker, 2012). The same is true with leadership opportunities. Teachers want to see their principals engaged and supportive of the teacher efforts. In doing so, teachers feel validated and valued for their time and leadership.

Professional Learning Communities

Most educators today have at least heard of Professional Learning Communities (PLCs) and their benefits, if operated properly. PLCs, according to DuFour and Eaker (1998) and Prenger, Poortman and Handelzalts (2018), are structures in which teachers can continue to grow and face the changing needs of students; in essence, the PLCs are organic bodies that learn as well. Teachers who operate in PLCs serve as content and instructional leaders in their own right.

Consider that the characteristics of PLCs, according to DuFour and Eaker (1998), which include a shared vision of learning with a shared inquiry about teaching practices that are questioned and altered to impact student learning. Teachers work in collaborative teams so that no one works in isolation, and they share an action orientation for continuous improvement that is results driven. Does this not sound like transformational leadership within the PLCs themselves and within the entire school organization?

Transformational leadership's goal is to afford employees the ability to solve problems and increase productivity through creativity and collective thought (Bass & Riggio, 2006; Bull, Martinez & Matute, 2019). Teachers in PLCs are solving learning problems, curriculum and assessment issues, all while exploring best practices in instructional strategies. Teachers are transformational leaders of learning when PLCs are utilized properly within a school.

When teachers in PLCs are given a focus for their meetings, and they understand how to achieve the goals through the proper training, teachers will exceed expectations and their self-efficacy will greatly expand. Teacher leaders are developed through PLC practice, and those same skills can be applied to other leadership structures such as a school's Leadership Team. Administrators should participate in PLC meetings, though they should never run them. Teachers should look to administrators for support and advice, but teachers are the content experts (think of their specific assets).

Administrators should know the work of the PLCs in their buildings through observation and reporting, but principals should let the teachers take the reins. As mentioned in a prior chapter, think of using set protocol for the meetings so that the meetings are run effectively and teachers' time is valued. Protocol for the meeting expectations should be clearly defined as well as protocol for different learning tasks, such as a Tuning Protocol that examines the relationship of the student work to the standards taught (McDonald, 2017). This assessment review practice serves to ensure that the student output is aligned to the teacher input.

In order to understand the progress and work of PLC's in a school building, principals should implement PLC feedback forms. These forms should be submitted to administration after a PLC. It is impossible for principals to attend all PLCs; however, the feedback forms provide an avenue for a principal to keep his thumb on the pulse of the work. Additionally, these feedback forms provide data that administrator can use to determine PD needs in the building. See figure 9.2 for a simple PLC Feedback Form.

When teachers are properly trained to function in PLCs and are given focus for their meetings, teacher productivity increases along with a sense of self-efficacy. This ability to problem-solve the learning issues that they and their students are experiencing gives teachers a sense of power and pride that

	Subject/Grade Level _____ Date_____
	Protocol Used:
PLC Feedback Form	Feedback from Protocol:
	Unanswered Questions:

Figure 9.2   PLC Feedback Form.

will propel them beyond any PD that can be provided for them. Teachers are the best resources for each other; they just need to be given the time to take advantage of each other's specific assets.

CONFIGURATION

So how does a principal set up a system for teacher leadership? The same way a principal sets up any system to begin, with planning and more planning. Consider all avenues of leadership needed in the school and map them out, like a strategic plan. See table 9.1 for a sample plan. Once the systems needed are identified, the principal needs to understand the resources needed for each system to include personnel, time, and funding.

Neglecting to examine each of these elements closely dooms a system to failure from the start. Teachers are inundated with unfunded and underappreciated mandates as it is. In fact, districts are inundated with the same and principals feel that frustration as well. Of course, principals cannot forget how they will show value to the teacher leaders through resources such as time and compensation. This step needs to be planned so it is not forgotten.

What other committees or groups may be needed other than a Leadership Team? Certainly, there is value in a Best Practices Committee that researches problems to derive proposed solutions to problems faced in a school. Data teams are often used to conduct needs assessments and present the problems to a Best Practices Committee. What other teams exist?

Each committee or team established should work together and feed one another so that the whole of the work does not rest on one group of teachers, which is typical. The norm is that there exists a small group of teachers who do all of the work along with administration. These teachers are often anchor teachers who are often revered and sometimes feared because of the influence they wield.

Intervention Teams may also be established that focus on monitoring at-risk students and reporting on interventions that work. The answer is multi-faceted. A principal has the ability to design a teacher leadership structure that fits the needs of the school and has the teacher leaders who are willing to do the work. Rather than relying on the few to complete the majority of the work, share the work and the leadership within the school.

The best way to tackle this task is to conduct a needs assessment based on the structures that currently exist in a school, and then work with the Leadership Team to establish the other groups needed. No one group should be inundated; there are enough teacher leaders to go around to get the work done. However, the flow of information needs to be decided as well as the reporting formats for each group.

PROGRESS MONITORING

Once all leadership systems are mapped and understood, the principal then needs to determine how each system will be evaluated for effectiveness. This step is often overlooked but is critical to success. How is a Leadership Team deemed to be successful? Is the work of the school getting done? Are teachers vested in school-based research to determine best practices? Are teachers satisfied with their representation? Each component has to be determined ahead of time and planned for in advance. See table 9.2 for an example.

Asking for teacher input in this planning process is important because they need to feel comfortable with the evaluation measure just as they need to understand that the evaluation is not an evaluation of a teacher, but of a system. This distinction is important to notate. Every system needs to be evaluated to determine what is working in the system and what is not. The system itself may need to be tweaked, and that is normal. What is not normal is to continue to do business in the same way and expect a different outcome. The latter method is not normal but is found to be typical, unfortunately.

Teachers, inherently, are nervous about evaluations; so, teacher leaders will have to trust that the principal is not evaluating a person but a practice. By giving teachers a voice in the evaluation methods and tools, they are likely to be more comfortable with the process. Not only do teacher leaders need to have voice in the planning process, but they also need to have voice in the evaluation results. What this means is that the teacher leaders need to be a part of the process in determining how to use the results. This type of shared leadership builds more confidence and trust in the system itself as well as administration.

Table 9.1 Sample Leadership Strategic Plan

Leadership Role	Purpose	Personnel	Time	Resources	Shown Value
Leadership Team	Develop programs and establish best practices in the school, work with school strategic plan	Anchor teachers mixed with new teachers selected by staff, guidance counselor, member of classified staff, all administration (Team of 12)	Once a month meeting	Stipend for Leadership Team members, funding for drinks/snacks for meetings and team garb	Recognition among staff, listed on school website, in school newsletters, etc. Team garb, Principal shares roles
School Improvement Council	Work with community to develop programs and support existing programs in school which constitute best practices, provide input from community and parents, work to create Strategic Plan and Report to the parents	Elected staff members, parents and community members, principal (six teachers, two parents, two community leaders, and principal)	Once a month meeting	Funding for food/drink for meetings, state training, and miscellaneous materials	Recognition among staff, listed on school website, in school newsletters, and so on. Principal shares roles
Department Chairs	Direct the work of the content departments as relates to strategic plan, provide feedback to leadership on progress monitoring, support the teachers within the department to include observation and feedback	Principal selected staff (one per department, two for larger departments)	Once a month meeting	Stipend for departmental chairs	Recognition among staff, listed on school website, in school newsletters, and so on. Principal attends meetings, One additional planning period (if feasible)

(Continued)

Table 9.1 Sample Leadership Strategic Plan (*Continued*)

Leadership Role	Purpose	Personnel	Time	Resources	Shown Value
MTSS Leads	Collect data on students referred to MTSS Teams, ensures all paperwork is completed prior to MTSS meetings and processes have been followed, schedules MTSS meetings	Volunteers among staff (one to two for each grade level)	Twice a month meetings	Stipends for MTSS Leads	Recognition among staff, listed on school website, in school newsletters, and so on. Team garb, Principal attends MTSS meetings
Robotics Lead	Coordinates all robotics team members, hold and directs practices and build season, coordinates business partners and industry partners to work with the team members, Attends at least two competitions with team	Science or math teacher interested in robotics (one to two depending on size of Robotics team).	Daily practices during build season and competition season	Stipend for Robotics Lead, Leadership Class for Robotics Leaders to coordinate schedules, marketing, volunteers, and so on.	Recognition among staff, on school website, principal newsletters, morning news segments, local newspapers, district website recognition, principal attends competitions and some practices

Benefits

Benefits of teacher leadership obviously extend to more than one arena. The first arena is teacher growth and satisfaction. Sharing leadership with teachers allows them to see all of the cogs in the wheel, which affords them to understand and develop the "how" and support the "why" of any school program. This understanding increases teacher morale and productivity. As a result, teachers learn and grow. Consequently, student achievement increases (Printy & Marks, 2006; Sebastian, Huang, & Allensworth, 2017).

Benefits to the staff, beyond improved effectiveness, include morale and retention. When teachers feel valued, as discussed before, their morale is higher and thus teacher motivation and retention rates follow (Muijs & Harris, 2003; Wang & Ho, 2019). In the current state of the national teacher shortage, teacher retention is a critical point. Another staff factor to consider is principal turnover and burnout. Principal leadership voids are becoming a shortage problem as well.

However, when leadership is shared, principals are at a lower risk of burning out. Remember, the job is bigger than any one person. Burnout predictors include exhaustion and lack of self-efficacy, or the belief the principal can do the job (Friedman, 1995). Well, no one can do it alone. Shared leadership builds self-efficacy.

Teacher leadership also has benefits to the school community. Think of a small community in which teachers are known to all, and what a teacher says travels quickly. Even in a larger community, people pay attention to what teachers are saying about their schools. If the teachers do not support a principal, the community knows about it. Students also talk about their teachers in the community. If teachers are not happy in their schools, students know it and share that information widely. With the advent of social media, news travels even faster than one can imagine.

Therefore, school community support is stronger when teacher leaders are developed and nourished in a school. Teacher satisfaction and morale, student achievement results, teacher and principal retention rates, and community support all increase with effective teacher leadership. Parents and businesses want to rally behind their community schools. Educators just need to give them a reason to do so. The impact of effective, shared leadership gives all stakeholders something to crow about.

HUMANISTIC APPROACH

Principals have to remember that teachers, as discussed earlier, all have different leadership needs. Different situations call for different leadership

Table 9.2 Progress Monitoring Systems of Teacher Leadership

Leadership Structure	Evaluation Component	Time	Personnel
Leadership Team	Teacher satisfaction survey	Twice a year	Survey sent by team leader
	Goals completed	Goals developed together prior to start of school year—report to faculty	Report to faculty by team leader
School improvement council	Elections	Held every year	Principal secretary sends out election forms
	Strategic plan	Developed in spring	All members work together
	Report to parents	Written in the spring	All members work together
	Goals completed	Goals developed together prior to start of school year	Report to school community by chair
	Satisfaction Survey	Once a year	Administered to faculty and school community by chair
Department chairs	Teacher satisfaction survey	Once a year	Administered to teachers by AP's for each department
	New teacher feedback	Fireside chats with admin once a month	Principal
	Progress monitoring tools	Departmental reports submitted once a month	Principal
	Data meetings to determine strengths and weaknesses in curriculum, PD needs, and so on	Once a month	Principal and all teachers
Robotics team lead	Enrollment of students in the program	Periodically through year, student attendance records	Team lead, principal observation
	Volunteer feedback survey	Once a year	Team lead, report to principal
	Industry partner survey	Once a year	Team lead, report to principal

approaches. For example, if a teacher, after support to ensure that the teacher understands the request, refuses to comply with a school policy, then a more direct leadership approach is needed. If a teacher is experienced and a leader in the school, then a more collaborative approach is needed when discussing a school issue. However, one must never forget that teachers are humans, and they have lives outside of school as well.

Students continually are surprised when they see their teachers in a local market or event outside of school, especially if that teacher is not in the attire normally associated with the teacher. Administrators need to envision those situations and remember that teachers have stresses outside of school, not just inside of school. The demands on teachers, like principals, have increased drastically over the years, and teaching is not an easy job. Teachers take work home with them almost daily, and their jobs impact their home lives as well.

Therefore, it is imperative that administrators deal with teachers with a humanistic psychological approach. Humanistic psychology is based on the tenant that people inherently want to perform well and make a positive impact through their free will. However, the whole person is more important than the sum of the parts (Buhler, 1971). In order to understand the whole person, administrators must look beyond the parts, which often is all an administrator sees. In essence, principals must understand a person's motivations and barriers to achievement for that person to become self-actualized.

Developing teacher leaders requires that principals inherently understand their staff. A principal would not assign a task to a teacher who was dealing with marital issues at home, just as a principal would not want to rely on the leadership of someone who was caring for a dying parent. Teachers want to lead, inherently, but each individual has a limit as to what he or she can handle. Principals need to recognize and appreciate those limits all while supporting teacher efforts. Teachers get burned out, just like principals do.

SYSTEMS APPROACH

To develop a systems approach to establishing leadership groups, principals need to determine needs first. As mentioned earlier, the flow of information and responsibilities of each group needs to be strategically planned. See figure 9.3 for a sample leadership system.

In the above diagram, the Leadership Team is the structure to which all information flows back. The box above the Leadership Team represents the agreed-upon duties of that group. Directly beneath the Leadership Team is where the principal and Leadership Team together determine the other leadership structures needed, such as a Best Practices Group or Data Teams, along

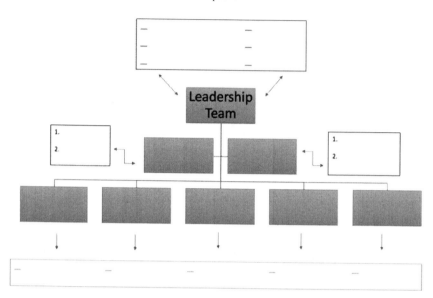

Figure 9.3   Sample Leadership System.

with their responsibilities. Notice their work is directed by the Leadership Team and the information obtained works back through the Leadership Team.

Directly beneath these other structures are where additional structures may exist. What about department chairs? Intervention Leads? Club sponsors? PLC leads? The point is that creating a systems structure with predesigned responsibilities and reporting procedures is critical for success. Each group should not work in isolation of each other; in this manner, transparency of mission and results are shared. Additionally, the work of the school can be effectively addressed. A principal can do just so much; however, the collective capacity of a school is impressive.

SUMMARY

Teacher leadership is essential for principals to nourish and develop, as the principal's job is bigger than any one person. Teachers inherently want to lead and feel confident about their specific assets (content knowledge and experiences). Principals must plan for teacher leadership systems in the building just as a principal plans for anything else. Strategically planning leadership systems includes the needs assessment, the parts of each system needed, the resources, the time, and evaluation components.

Teachers should be included in the planning process as they will see the need for the system as well as feel comfortable with the evaluation of the system. It is critical that teachers understand the evaluation of a leadership system is not an evaluation of a teacher but of the system itself. Leadership systems include traditional systems like Leadership Teams and school improvement councils but extend to student groups such as athletics and content area groups. Teacher PLCs and other committees establish teacher leadership in the building while advancing a school's vision.

Lastly, principals must remember to use a humanistic approach when developing and establishing teacher leadership systems. Even though teachers inherently want to achieve, they also have lives outside of school. Therefore, it is important to consider the whole person before addressing teachers for leadership roles. Teachers can burn out just like principals do.

A PIECE AT A TIME

- What is a teacher's specific asset?
- How can a principal show support for teacher leadership?
- How does a school benefit from teacher leadership? Name at least three ways.
- What are different avenues for teacher leadership?
- How does a principal plan for teacher leadership?
- What elements must be included in the plan?
- What approach should principals take when developing teacher leaders and why?

REFERENCES

Bass, B. & Riggio, R. (2006). *Transformational leadership.* Mahwah, NJ: Erlbaum Associates Publishing.

Buhler, C. (1971). Basic theoretical concepts of humanistic psychology. *American Psychologist, 26*(4), 378–86.

Bull, I., Martinez, E. & Matute, J. (2019). Transformational leadership and employee performance: The role of identification, engagement and proactive personality. *International Journal of Hospitality Management, 77,* 64–75.

DuFour, R. & Eaker, R. (1998). *Professional communities at cork: Best practices for enhancing student achievement.* Bloomington, IN: Solution Tree Press.

Eagly, A. H. & Johannesen-Schmidt, M. C. (2001). The leadership styles of men and women. *Journal of Social Issues, 7*(4), 781–97.

Eagly, A. H., Wood, W., & Diekman, A. B. (2000). Social role theory of sex differences and similarities: A current appraisal. In T. Eckes and H. M. Trautner (Eds.), *The developmental social psychology of gender* (pp. 123–74). Mahwah, NJ: Erlbaum.

Friedman, I. (1995). School principal burnout: The concept and its components. *Journal of Organizational Behavior, 16*(2), 191–98.

Kernis, M. H. (2003). Toward a conceptualization of optimal self-esteem. *Psychological Inquiry, 14,* 1–26.

Lindenberg, S. (1990). Homo socio-oeconomicus: The emergence of a general model of man in the social sciences. *Journal of Institutional and Theoretical Economics, 146,* 727–48.

Lindenberg, S. (1996). Transaction cost economics and beyond. In J. Groenewegen (Ed.), *Short-term prevalence, social approval, and the governance of employment* (pp. 129–47). Norwell, MASS: Kluwer Academic Publishers.

Maslow, A. H. (1970). *Motivation and personality* (2nd ed.). New York: Harper and Row.

McDonald, J. (2017). Tuning protocol. Retrieved from https://www.schoolreforminitiative.org/download/tuning-protocol/.

Muijs, D. & Harris, A. (2003). Teacher leadership—Improvement through empowerment?: An overview of the literature. *Educational Management & Administration, 31*(4), 437–48.

Norman, S., Avolio, B., & Luthans, F. (2010). The impact of positivity and transparency on trust in leaders and their perceived effectiveness. *The Leadership Quarterly, 21*(3), 350–64.

Prenger, R., Poortman, C., & Handelzalts, A. (2019). The effects of networked professional learning communities. *Journal of Teacher Education, 70*(5), 441–52.

Printy, S. & Marks, M. (2006). Shared leadership for teacher and student learning. *Theory into Practice, 45*(2), 125–32.

Quinn, D. M. (2002). The impact of principal leadership behaviors on instructional practice and student engagement. *Journal of Educational Administration, 40*(5), 447–67.

Ridgeway, C. L. (1997). Interaction and the conservation of gender inequality: Considering employment. *American Sociological Review, 62,* 218–35.

Sebastian, J., Huang, H., & Allensworth, E. (2017). Examining integrated leadership systems in high schools: Connecting principal and teacher leadership to organizational processes and student outcomes. *School Effectiveness and School Improvement, 28*(3), 463–88.

Wang, M. & Ho, D. (2019). A quest for teacher leadership in the twenty-first century-emegerging themes for future research. *International Journal of Educational Management, 34*(2), 354–72.

Whitaker, B. (2012). Instructional leadership and principal visibility. *The Clearinghouse: A Journal of Educational Strategies, Issues, and Ideas, 70*(3), 155–56.

Conclusion

Change is a constant. This may seem like an oxymoron, but it is a universal truth. Schools are certainly not immune to the changes societies face, as schools reflect the communities in which they reside. Administrators have to lead and manage schools through the myriad of changes that are thrown their way, all while ensuring that students, the clientele, are properly prepared for the next step. Books 1 and 2 together are designed to help those administrators design the systems needed to maximize effectiveness.

Throughout this book, the analogy used to suggest a systems design has been the stages of construction when building a schoolhouse, with the foundation as the systems lens needed to organize the work of schools. The placement of the first two major systems is not accidental, as each one serves a function that helps to support the other. In figure C.1, you will see the four major systems needed.

The system of curriculum and instruction provides the framing for the schoolhouse, as this system gives us our purpose, our form. The vertical supports are teacher supports, and these supports run parallel with curriculum and instruction. Naturally, these two systems comprise the *Putting the Pieces Together* book.

As both systems must work in concert to support and give direction to student support systems, the second book *The Final Pieces* will address the expansive student support system needed to create an environment best suited to student success. Additionally, the culture system will be represented in the next volume as well. After all, culture does not happen in a vacuum; it is developed, either with intent or not.

Imagine the builder who runs out of money on a housing project. The outer walls and some supports are up, but the rest of the support system as well as

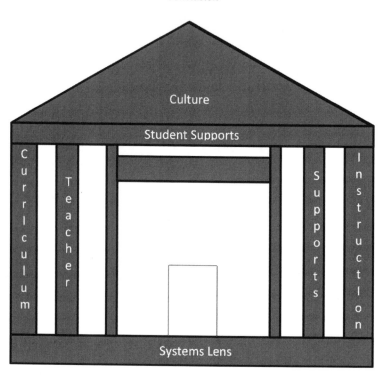

Figure C.1   A Systems Approach to School Leadership.

the roof is incomplete. What happens to that housing project? It falls in disrepair quickly due to weather and other elements. As in represented in both books, all four systems must work in concert, or the school system designed for success is incomplete, and therefore are susceptible to the bombardment of elements that exist today which can cause erosion and disrepair. See you in the second book!

About the Author

Dr. Lee Westberry has over twenty years' experience as a school administrator. She has served as a middle school principal, a high school principal, and a district supervisor in more than one capacity. Prior to serving as an administrator, Dr. Westberry was an English teacher in more than one school.

Most recently, Dr. Westberry serves as the Educational Leadership Program coordinator and assistant professor of Educational Leadership in the Zucker Family School of Education at The Citadel in Charleston, SC. In addition to teaching classes in the master's program and Educational Specialist program, Dr. Westberry also supports principal leaders in the form of Principal Service. In this capacity, Dr. Westberry travels across the state to provide professional learning experiences for sitting principals.

Dr. Westberry is also the CEO of the FLIP Educational Group, LLC (Focused Leadership in Practice), which serves to consult with districts and schools, providing training for teaching staffs, instructional coaches, and principals where needed.

In addition to her passion for education, Dr. Westberry has a passion for her family. Married for over twenty-eight years to her high school sweetheart, Dr. Westberry strives to be the best wife to Danny and mother to her two smart and beautiful daughters, Warner and Sophie.